THE NIGHT
THE ANGELS CAME

MIRACLES OF PROTECTION AND PROVISION IN BURUNDI

Chrissie Chapman

MONARCH
BOOKS

Oxford, UK & Grand Rapids, Michigan, USA

Published by Monarch Books
an imprint of
Lion Hudson plc
Wilkinson House, Jordan Hill Road,
Oxford OX2 8DR, England
Email: monarch@lionhudson.com
www.lionhudson.com/monarch

ISBN 978 0 85721 722 6
e-ISBN 978 0 85721 723 3

First edition 2016

Acknowledgments
Unless otherwise noted Scripture quotations taken from the *Holy Bible,
New Living Translation*, copyright © 1996, 2004, 2007 by Tyndale House
Foundation. Used by permission of Tyndale House Publishers, Inc., Carol
Stream, Illinois 60188. All rights reserved.
Scripture quotations marked NIV are taken from the *Holy Bible, New
International Version*, copyright © 1973, 1978, 1984 International Bible
Society. Used by permission of Hodder & Stoughton, a member of the
Hodder Headline Group. All rights reserved. 'NIV' is a trademark of
International Bible Society. UK trademark number 1448790.
Scripture quotations marked NKJV are taken from the New King James
Version. Copyright © 1982 by Thomas Nelson, Inc. Used by permission.
All right reserved.
Extract pp. 25–26 taken from the song "God Will Make a Way" by Don
Moen. Copyright © 1990 Integrity's Hosanna! Music. Adm. By Capitol
CMG Publishing excl. UK, adm. By Integrity Music, part of the David C
Cook family, songs@integritymusic.com Used with permission.

A catalogue record for this book is available from the British Library

Printed and bound in the UK, January 2016, LH26

This book is dedicated to my children Lydia, Hannah, and Benjamin, and to every child whom God has entrusted into my care at CRIB. Also to Rosa and Deo, who have served us faithfully with an abundance of love, joy, and humility.

CONTENTS

FOREWORD

I t is an honour and a privilege to write a foreword for this book. I have known Chrissie Chapman for many years, and count her as one of my heroes.

There is one story that sums up why I see her as a hero. The setting is Chrissie's house and a group of armed men had taken charge of it. They were holding Chrissie at gunpoint, away from her orphan children. Hearing a shot from another room was too much for Chrissie. Without giving it a second thought, she charged out of the room like a mother bear whose cubs are in danger. The armed men, also alarmed by the shot, fled.

Chrissie has suffered from ill health and come close to death a number of times. On one occasion, she was hospitalized in south London for surgery but caught one of those hospital bugs as well. She was not expected to live. I was on my way back home to Vancouver, but when I heard of Chrissie's state, I decided to leave early. At Heathrow, I placed my luggage in a container and caught a train to

Paddington, then the underground and a bus to reach the hospital. When I walked into her ward, Chrissie was somewhat delirious and thought she was now in heaven and that I was an angel. She soon discovered I was no such being and became quite alert and I was able to pray for her. That was not the only time she fought for her life, however, throughout she continued to seek and serve God in Burundi following such challenges.

Furthermore, even as Burundi has suffered war a number of times, as is the case at this present moment, Chrissie continues to stand by her post, taking risks when others have left. This is the reason why Chrissie is one of my missionary heroes.

Barney Coombs
International Leader, Salt and Light Ministries

ACKNOWLEDGMENTS

This book would not have been possible without the agreement of the children in the CRIB home and the team of people who work with me. Thank you for allowing me to tell your stories.

My friend Carleen Higgs has spent many hours typing, correcting, and editing the manuscript. I am so grateful for all the help and advice you have given me.

I have also greatly appreciated the assistance of my friend Dr Swee Lip Quek in the editing of the book. Thank you for encouraging me to finally put pen to paper.

I could not have written this book without all of their encouragement and commitment to help. I am greatly in their debt.

Lastly, I would like to thank my three wonderful children Lydia, Hannah, and Benjamin Chapman. Thank you for your cooperation with the writing of this book and allowing me to include your stories. I am a very proud mother.

WHY I WROTE THIS BOOK

I have lived and worked in Burundi for twenty-five years. It is a Third World country and they say that it ranks as the second poorest country in the world.

I went to Burundi as a medical missionary to open a maternity clinic and dispensary in a rural area of the country. I had been there just three years when a coup was declared and the country descended into a state of civil war for thirteen years. During that time, God directed me to work with orphans and widows. I started a centre for abandoned babies and traumatized children and I have been in a very privileged position of seeing the Lord doing the most amazing miracles in the lives of people who have lost every material possession. Many have lost family members and some their entire family.

For years, I have shared their stories as I have travelled and spoken in churches and Christian camps in England, Canada and America. Over and over again, many people have said to me that I should write a book detailing my experiences.

I feel that now is the time. There is a story to be told about the faithfulness and grace of God. The healing power of Jesus is still at work today. I have seen and experienced many miracles and feel it is long overdue that I start to document some of these events I have been privileged enough to witness.

My life has been the most incredible journey. I have been given the opportunity to walk a path in life which has been full of miraculous signs and wonders which proves the tremendous compassion, power and faithfulness of God. This is what I want to share. I believe that this book will be a great encouragement to many people. I am convinced that God can use these testimonies and stories to unleash a surge of faith. Consequently, this book will uplift and edify Christians the world over. It will also be directed to non-Christians to demonstrate that God, though almighty, loves and cares for them as individuals, more than they can possibly imagine. This book will debunk the notion that God is no longer in the business of miracles.

BURUNDI

The small heart-shaped country of Burundi is situated in the central eastern part of Africa, which is also known as the African Great Lakes region. Although Burundi is referred to as landlocked, its capital city, Bujumbura, sits adjacent to the world's second deepest lake, Lake Tanganyika.

Burundi borders several other countries: Rwanda to the north, Tanzania to the south and east, and the Democratic Republic of Congo on the western side of Lake Tanganyika.

With a population of around 10.4 million people,[1] Burundi is ranked as the world's second poorest country with 65 per cent of the population living below the poverty line.[2] Burundi has a very young population with approximately 47 per cent aged fourteen years and under and 3 per cent aged sixty-five and over.[3] It has the second largest population density in Africa with most people living on farms and surviving by growing their own crops. The population is made up of three ethnic groups: Hutu, Tutsi, and Batwa. Their official languages are Kirundi and French,

1 As per www.bbc.co.uk/news/world-africa-13085064
2 www.africaw.com/major-problems-facing-burundi-today
3 www.worldrover.com/vital/burundi.html

and more recently English, which is now taught in most schools in Bujumbura.

In 1993, Burundi came to the world's attention when, as a result of longstanding ethnic tensions, it experienced a brutal and prolonged civil war which lasted approximately thirteen years and which, it is estimated, claimed around 300,000 lives.

From 2006 to 2015, Burundi experienced a time of relative peace and stability. However, in April 2015, once again this beautiful country saw an explosion of serious political unrest and another civil war became a very real possibility.

CHAPTER 1

THE SOUND OF SILENCE

In the stifling African heat, the newborn infant's cry came, at first, falteringly, then with healthy gusto. I felt a profound sense of exhilaration coupled with utter relief when it sunk in that the first delivery in our wonderful new clinic had been straightforward and complication free. We were on our way!

I had waved goodbye to the UK in the autumn of 1990 for the purpose of opening and running a maternity clinic and dispensary in Burundi. I thought that this project would probably take me about two years and I arrived ready to serve God, complete with all kinds of medical instruments in tow for the clinic. Within a few weeks of my arrival, several additional boxes of supplies I had collected while working at a maternity hospital in the UK arrived via airfreight. Setting up a clinic from scratch was an exciting but rather daunting task for me, even though I had previously worked as a midwife in several prestigious hospitals in England. In a medical emergency, I was used to pressing a red panic button, following which the duty doctors would arrive within minutes and take control of the situation. However, here I was in Burundi with no red button and no doctors on hand to help – and to add to the mix, no running water or electricity.

As I walked through the doors of the little building that was going to be my clinic, it hit me just how much work it was going to take to get this clinic up and running, especially as I was organizing everything myself. First, I had to find workmen to clear the roof of the nesting bats that had destroyed the ceiling, and then clean and paint the whole place. It then took me weeks to find a carpenter to make beds and cribs for the babies, and a tailor to produce sheets and curtains to separate the beds. There were days when I seriously thought we would never ever open the clinic, let alone perform any medical procedures. But here we were with our first healthy new arrival safely in the arms of his relieved mother.

It had never occurred to me that God might have other plans for me. As I say, I had reckoned on being in Burundi for a couple of years and then returning to the UK. It had also never crossed my mind that I would be doing anything else other than delivering babies. However, it was only a few months after my arrival in Burundi that I began to realize that the Lord in His great wisdom doesn't reveal too much too soon.

Within two days of my arrival in Burundi, a young girl, about seventeen years old, came to see me to ask if I would give her a job as my house worker. Strapped to her back she had a baby girl who was sixteen months old but who was very small: she looked more like a twelve-month-old baby. Both mother and child looked quite hungry and unkempt, and obviously in need of help. My heart went out to both of them and I accepted this young girl and her tiny daughter as my house girl. The baby's name was Lydia. Although she was small, nervous, and very timid, for me it was love at first sight. This tiny bundle instantly made her way into my heart and within a few weeks it was like watching a little rosebud opening up. She started to smile and babble and although still very timorous, she loved cuddles. Her mother was a good worker with a bubbly personality; very likeable but there was a certain restlessness about her. She found it very hard to stay home and take care of Lydia and would often wander off and leave her alone sleeping or would simply forget to feed her. We were living in quite an isolated area on top of a mountain, which meant it took quite a while to get into the city or to have a life outside where we lived.

One day the house worker had a day off. She took Lydia with her, but didn't return. A few days passed and I heard that they were living in a derelict house in the city and that Lydia was very sick. I immediately went and found them. I could see that this young mum was not able to take care of Lydia and she asked if I could take her so that Lydia might have a reasonable chance of having a good life. It was patently clear that she couldn't cope with the responsibility of this child and, at seventeen years old, she was only really a child herself. I was convinced that if Lydia stayed with her she would not survive. At that moment, I scooped this small, sad bundle into my arms. She was already in my heart and I took her into my home. It was on this day that I realized that maybe I was going to be in Burundi longer than I had first anticipated.

I found another house girl who helped me look after Lydia while I was at the clinic. Life was busy: the maternity clinic was fully operational and before long, with the help of two other nurses who came up from the city, we started an antenatal clinic one morning a week. We also set up a vaccination clinic for babies. This brought additional frustrations because the vaccines had to be kept in a fridge and with no electricity this was a major problem. However, we managed to get hold of a paraffin fridge which worked reasonably well, but I have vivid memories of finding this "beast" bellowing thick, black smoke into the office where it was kept. It would often take me a couple of hours to re-trim the wick and get it working again, and of course then having to wash the inky soot off my desk and the walls. "The joys of living in Africa" became my daily catchphrase and confession, especially in the middle of the night. Eventually we acquired a generator, which meant we could replace the paraffin lamps which hung on the intravenous drip stands and replace them with reliable electric lights. What a glorious day that was – to be able to see the babies who were being delivered and not to be squinting in the dim light of the ancient paraffin lamps!

After about three months the dispensary opened, along with a small laboratory attached to it, and my little clinic became a very busy and successful centre. Fortunately I lived just a five minute walk away. There was also a Bible-training centre on the property and I was blessed by their college students coming to the clinic waiting area every morning to sing and pray for the patients sitting in the waiting room. It was a joy to see the clinic successfully helping the local people. It was especially gratifying for me to see healthy babies going home with happy mothers. It was an amazing and very fulfilling experience.

In February 1993 a friend contacted me to tell me about some twin girls, just six weeks old, whose mother had died after giving birth to them. Their father had died a few weeks prior to them being born. An aunt was left trying to look after them and her own child while at the same time working full-time as a nanny for an American family.

I had recently shared with this friend a dream I had experienced. A couple of months prior to this conversation, I had woken up early in the morning and sat bolt upright in bed with the full impact of the dream. I was holding a baby boy. It was so real was that I could almost feel the baby's breath on my neck. I felt so strongly that God was going to give me this little boy. I started to collect baby clothes and went to talk to my friends Graham and Sarah White, who had lived in Burundi for many years and who were responsible for running and pastoring an English-speaking fellowship which I attended. I asked Sarah to let me know if anyone turned up on her doorstep with a baby boy. While there was no baby boy at that moment, these two little girls turned up who were not in a particularly healthy state, and I felt nothing but compassion when I saw them. I could not refuse to help just because this was not the baby boy I had seen in my dream. As my friend Chris, who was visiting from the UK for six weeks, offered to help, I took the twin girls but was informed that they had a grandfather who would take them back into the family when they were old enough to eat solids – in about twelve to fifteen months time. It was hard work: Lydia was almost four and attending nursery school in the mornings at that point. I was very busy at the clinic and in those early stages I was the only one able to cover the night shifts. Babies do love to be born in the middle of the night! I could never have survived those first few weeks without the help of Chris! The twins were six weeks old when they came to me and it was only a matter of days after taking them in that I realized they were both quite weak and unwell. They had not been given names. In Burundi, twins are often called *bukuru* and *botoyi*, which simply means "twin one" and "twin two". I decided to give them names. Twin one, the darker chubbier baby, I called Hannah, and twin two, the smaller and very pale baby, I called Deborah. Hannah was sick after every feed and was always restless and hungry. Deborah was never hungry and seemed very weak.

The day came when I had to take them both to hospital in the city to see a paediatrician and find out what was ailing them. When the doctor saw them, he showed particular concern for Deborah, and decided to admit them both into the hospital for intravenous fluids and further tests. Deborah had pneumonia; she improved with a course of antibiotics but remained weak. Hannah didn't appear to be as ill as her twin, but continued to regurgitate all her feeds. A week later I was called into the doctor's office to be told that the blood tests confirmed that both babies were HIV positive. It was thought that their parents had probably died because of AIDS-related illnesses and in all probability the twins were condemned to the same fate. I had only had the babies a month when I got this news but I was utterly devastated. I had already fallen in love with them and had wondered how I would ever pass them back to their grandfather in the future.

I managed to take the girls home. After Chris left to go back to the UK I continued to juggle life with a four-year-old, two sick babies, and a very busy clinic to run. I remember carrying the girls in wicker Moses baskets to the clinic night after night when I was called to perform deliveries. Relatives of the patients watched my girls for me when I was busy delivering new life but the desperate irony remained that the life of my precious girls was slowly seeping out of them.

Graham and Sarah White, who ran the English-speaking church, were a great support and I asked them to pray for the babies and to dedicate them when they were about three months old. Hannah was a fighter. Deborah continued to get weaker and weaker until, on Good Friday 1993, she went to be with the Lord. We had a small funeral service for her the next day, on Holy Saturday. It was a special time as we committed her into the arms of the Lord and remembered that we were also celebrating that Jesus rose from the dead so that we might experience eternal life with Him. What a comfort at that time. I knew that Deborah was safe in the arms of Jesus and she was now gloriously healed and free.

Life went on as busy as ever. Hannah continued to reject most of her feeds and often had chesty coughs. She was, despite all her health challenges, quite a placid baby. It was several months later when Hannah was eight months old that something happened that changed both of our lives.

I had had a particularly busy week. One night I delivered no less than nine babies between midnight and 7 a.m. I was trying to keep going at this pace, being up almost every night either at the clinic or attempting to get Hannah to keep some food down. One morning I came home from the clinic at around 3 a.m. I sat down with a baby bottle and Hannah in my arms. I was exhausted and feeling at the end of my tether. I felt I didn't have the strength to get through another day. I turned on a Don Moen music tape and closed my eyes as the song he was singing seemed to permeate my being;

> *God will make a way*
> *Where there seems to be no way*

He works in ways we cannot see
He will make a way for me.

He will be my guide
Hold me closely to His side
With love and strength for each new day
He will make a way, He will make a way.

It was as if Jesus had walked into the room in my little mud house on top of the mountain in the middle of Africa; there were hot and exhausted tears running down my face. I was afraid to open my eyes because it felt as if I had been transported to a wonderful sandy beach: it was as if the warm rays of the sun were beating down on me and the sea breeze was washing over me and my baby girl. I never wanted this feeling to go. The presence of the Holy Spirit at that moment was life-changing. I encountered the love of the Father in a way I had never known before. I fell asleep with Hannah asleep in my arms. I think I must have slept for about three hours because when I opened my eyes it was 6.30 a.m. and the morning rays of sunlight were beaming in through the window. For the first time ever, Hannah had finished her bottle without throwing up on me. She seemed somehow different: content and happy in a new way. Over the days that followed, I couldn't believe how she drank and ate with a new-found appetite and enthusiasm for food and for life. From that night, Hannah never looked back – she positively thrived.

Later, when Hannah was one, I had her retested for HIV. This time the result came back negative. Just to be sure, three months later, when she was fifteen months old, I had her tested again. Once again the results came back negative. She was healed, she was whole, she was healthy, and Jesus had done it.

Today, Hannah is twenty-two and studying law at a prestigious university in London. In the end, I didn't hand my tiny miracle baby back to her old grandfather. In fact, it was several years after their arrival that we found he was still alive and living in Rwanda. I adopted Hannah (in Burundi, adoption is possible after twelve months in the case of abandonment) and her goal today is to work in an area where she can help others who are in a place of disadvantage. Her desire is to make a difference with the life Jesus has given back to her. Saved "for such a time as this" (Esther 4:14, NIV).

Life was good. The clinic and dispensary were going well. Lydia was enjoying nursery school; Hannah was beginning to thrive and mercifully sleeping through the night. For a couple of months in 1993 I found a new lease of life. Then October arrived and with it, a coup.

On the morning of 21 October, Burundi woke up to the sound of silence. We were used to the familiar hustle and bustle of people on their way to market before sunrise, with their goats, cows, and chickens and all the subsequent noise they generated. On this particular day, not one person or radio could be heard: a clear sign to those who had lived long enough in Burundi to know that this unnatural silence did not signal something good. Something, in fact, was very wrong. Later that morning, our worst fears were realized when we heard from some neighbours that there had been a coup. Burundi was at war.

It was some time later that we heard that the newly elected president, who had only been in office for a few months, had been assassinated. In the hours, days, and weeks that followed, we were surrounded by absolute chaos. It was estimated that 300,000 people were killed in the conflict that followed. The situation in which I found myself was one for which no Bible school or training college could ever have prepared me.

My first priority was to try and get my children and as many of the twelve team members as possible off the mountain. We sent one of our local house boys as a runner with notes we had written to our friends in the town of Bujumbura, who by now realized that we were essentially stranded on the mountain. After some discussion and prayer, we sent a note to ask some of our friends to drive to the bottom of the mountain to rescue us before the road became completely impassable. We quickly packed the Land Cruiser that we used as our ambulance, with Lydia, Hannah, and the rest of the workers, and David Ndaruhutse (the director of the centre and our ministry, and the founder of African Revival Ministries under whom our clinic was established) drove the vehicle in a terrifying dash down the mountain. When we reached the bottom, the children were swiftly handed over to friends and the rest of the team were able to quickly escape. Although there was still a lot of shooting and violence, it was safer for the children to be in the city, and at that moment, I entrusted them to the Father's care.

David Ndaruhutse and I returned to the mountain. Patients were still coming to the clinic for medical help and the healing centre had some vulnerable mentally challenged patients that needed care. We had nowhere to send them in the city and no one to accompany them to ensure their safety. David and I felt that for the moment we should just take it a day at a time and see what unfolded as the week progressed. We could offer help where we could at the clinic while not really knowing what was around the corner.

Looking back, I can see that I was completely naive in that situation. There I was thinking that within a few days everything would settle down and revert to normality and that my children and the rest of our team would return to us again very soon. Wow! Was I mistaken! I had no idea of what would unfold in the weeks and months that followed. I had no concept at all that the next two weeks were going to be the last I would live and work on that mountain. In fact it would be about another fifteen years before I ever returned to see the remains of the clinic that I had started, and the ruins of my former home. I had absolutely no idea.

In normal times, our food was brought up on a daily basis from the town. Because of the heat, and with no fridges, it was necessary to buy supplies of fresh food, especially meat and vegetables, each day. Obtaining water was also a challenge since the nearest standpipe was situated about two miles away. Each day our driver would collect barrels of water on his way back from market and bring them back. However, in our present predicament we were stuck with hardly any food – just a couple of kilos of beans and rice – and water was in short supply. Since it was the rainy season we managed to collect rainwater for everyday use for cleaning and washing ourselves, but to obtain water to make tea we had to send one of our boys to run up, then down, and then across to the other side of the mountain to the nearest standpipe to bring back water we could boil. However, I did have a Christmas cake in my kitchen that my good friend Dave Pailthorpe from the UK had made and had sent out to me. It came in very handy as we ate that cake for breakfast, lunch, and tea for three days running! I have never tasted cake so good since.

Patients continued to come to the clinic, but usually after sunset when it was dark, around 6.30 in the evening. In those uncertain days, I felt out of my depth when dealing with some of the medical emergencies that arrived either at the clinic or on my doorstep. Expectant mothers turned up every night, but only the ones who had developed complications. Usually by the time they arrived, the complications had become even more complicated. It was impossibly stressful, coupled with the road now being completely impassable and fighting and shooting going on around us. During the nights it was impossible to even think about trying to transfer any patients who were too complex for me to deal with. For five nights in a row I delivered stillborn babies. It was heart-rending. Other patients came with all sorts of injuries and illnesses. I kept a book in my office called *Where There is No Doctor*. It catalogued all sorts of medical conditions and diseases with a description at the end of each chapter on how to treat the complaint. The last paragraph always seemed to give the same advice: if you have done all that is advised and there is no improvement, go to your nearest clinic or doctor. A lot of help that was to me, since I *was* the clinic and the doctor!

To this day I am still amazed at how God gave me the strength, the wisdom, and the guidance to know how to cope and deal with every situation that presented itself. It always happened that when I was too tired to even think straight, there was a lull in the storm, and for several hours at a time, nobody would come near the clinic or to my door. It was as if God kept the people back and gave me a supernatural ability to be able to close my eyes and to stop thinking and worrying about what would next come through the door. I often lay down and slept and then woke up just a couple of hours later feeling refreshed as if I had had a good night's sleep. I didn't realize at the time that I was experiencing miracles every day: sleep, peace, and wisdom to know what to do without panic. It was not for a while that I could appreciate how much grace God had poured out over me, David, and the other workers who had stayed to help. I never realized just how blessed I was to experience all this when the rest of the country was gripped with crippling fear as the war raged around us.

In our second week trapped on that mountain, we came to realize that the situation was escalating rather than improving. With grieving hearts, we heard news from across the country of the devastation, destruction, and general madness that ensued. However, we prayed and although we couldn't quite work out how, we felt God was going to make a way for us to be rescued and moved from that place.

It happened early one morning. I had been at the clinic with a young woman all night. She was in labour and having her first child. She had arrived in the early hours of the morning, having been in labour all day. It didn't take me too long to realize we had problems. The baby was breach: bottom first instead of the more usual way of being head first. However, one of the baby's legs had somehow unflexed and one small foot was visible. The mother was of course extremely distressed, having been in pain for hours with severe contractions. She was tired and weak. The baby was still alive with a strong, but very slow, heartbeat. I didn't know what to do. There was no red panic button, no doctor, and no sterile operating theatre she could be taken to in an attempt to save the mother's life and the life of her baby. I cried and I prayed and I cried again, but this time my cries were directed to heaven: "Jesus, if ever we needed your help, it is now! Right now, right here in the middle of this raging war and gunfire." The rage I was experiencing inside my head completely shut out everything else. I simply couldn't face delivering another dead baby. I decided to sedate the mother to try and help her relax. I ran down to the healing centre to pour out all my grief on David. A decision was made on the spot. He ran to the neighbourhood's zone leader, who knew us very well, and explained the situation. To this day, I still do not know how it happened but people from all the surrounding areas appeared bringing stones and wood and anything else they could find. They began to repair the road to make it possible for us to drive down to the hospital in the city with this lady. It took two hours to repair over two miles of road – literally hundreds of people from near and far lined the roads as I set off down the mountain. They waved and cried out that they would wait for me to return.

I arrived at the hospital around 6 a.m., dropped off my patient and decided to take a detour on my way back to the mountain. I quickly made my way to my friends' house to hug Lydia and Hannah who were staying with them. I then called to greet a doctor friend and before I knew what was happening, after half an hour, and a few phone calls, several cars appeared with friends waiting to escort me back up the mountain. The idea was that they would help me pack up as much as we could and then evacuate David and the rest of the team who remained on the mountain. I could do nothing but sit with my mouth open and watch as quickly and efficiently my dear friends packed up so many things from the house and the clinic. Using the sheets from the beds in the clinic, one friend very carefully packed a set of small china teapots I had on display on a shelf in my sitting room (in an attempt to make my little mud house homely!). Amazingly, only one lid got broken in that evacuation!

We knew that as soon as we left, anything remaining would be looted and never seen again. At that point, it felt so good to be alive, nothing else seemed to matter much at all. Once again, the local people lined the road and for the last time, we drove down the mountain with our heads held high and tears flowing down our cheeks as our neighbours begged and implored that one day we would return home. Sadly that day was never to come.

It was about a year later that a small team of nationals, nurses and one laboratory man who had worked with me from the opening of the dispensary, decided to risk going back to reopen the clinic and try to help where they could. The war was still raging and it was dangerous to return there. The day came when some gunmen rounded up all the clinic staff, lined them up, and shot them. The only survivor was the laboratory worker. He fell down when the shooting began and was thought to be dead, lying quietly until all was clear. He lived to tell the tale.

There were many like him who, when the country eventually came back into a place of relative peace, could tell their own stories of how God protected and provided for them in amazing and miraculous ways.

I can see how God's hand was on me and on the team He put with me. There are many things we don't understand; many questions still unanswered but all I can do is to give testimony to what I saw and what I experienced myself. In those weeks when the war first started I felt everything I had experienced up to that point in my life had been in preparation for what I was living through in those tumultuous times.

I think the one person who God used to speak into my life and provoke me to reach out to Jesus in ways I had never really comprehended before was David. He was, without doubt, one of the most amazing men of God I have ever met. In the middle of all the chaos that we lived through, I had an encounter that I will never forget when, one evening, we had visitors.

CHAPTER 2

THE NIGHT
THE ANGELS CAME

I have never felt so close to God as I did on that mountain. At night, the moon sometimes looked like a luminous light bulb suspended in the sky. With the lack of pollution, we could see the stars very distinctly and the skies were alight with God's exquisite handiwork: awesome beauty in the midst of carnage.

One evening, David and I were sitting on the front doorstep of my small mud house, gazing at the moon and the stars and wondering what the future held. Gunfire sounded all around us and we could hear crying and terrified screaming coming from the hills. You could feel and almost touch the terror in those screams. As we sat praying and crying out to God for His help, peace, and protection, David suddenly stood up and began to praise God. He was saying over and over, "Thank you, Jesus, thank you, Jesus." He cried out to me, "Chrissie, just look on the walls." I couldn't see anything and didn't know what he was talking about. David put his hands on my eyes and prayed that God would open my eyes to see what he was seeing. As I opened my eyes, I saw dozens of huge angels standing shoulder to shoulder on top of the six-foot high wall that surrounded the perimeter of our healing centre. These strong, shining heavenly beings clothed in full armour with gleaming breastplates were standing on top of the wall in a complete circle with their backs to us, looking outward. They looked so huge and strong. I was filled with so much awe that every bit of fear drained out of my body and could no longer touch me.

From that moment, and for the next twelve years during which the war continued, I have never experienced nor felt fear for my life. That experience and that sense of awe have remained with me for over twenty years now, in what has turned out to be a most incredible and amazing journey!

At that point my mind raced back to other occasions when I had had supernatural encounters with God. I had never seen an angel before but I had experienced feelings of overwhelming peace at other times in His presence. Several years prior to my and David's vision, while I was in the UK, I had been healed when God had given me two healthy new lungs in my body to the amazement of the doctors. The other occasion had occurred only a few weeks before seeing the angels: that time when I had felt the tangible presence of the Holy Spirit in my room, when healing and wholeness had been brought to Hannah. On both of these occasions, the feeling was the same overwhelming sense of holiness, coupled with my unwillingness to move out of or disturb the profound and beautiful presence of God. At these times I was left with a sense of wonder and an indisputable knowledge that God was God and Jesus was Lord and there was absolutely nothing that could touch me while in His presence. I became so aware that there is another dimension in the spiritual world that is not seen or even noticeable on a day-to-day basis. I experienced an absolute certainty that nothing is impossible for Him if only we can believe that this is the case.

The perimeter of the wall around the healing centre was about a quarter of a mile long and those heavenly beings stood shoulder to shoulder with no space between each one. We did not see their faces; they seemed to be dressed in armour with golden breastplates. They were tall, appearing like giants, yet bringing no sense of fear, only unspeakable awe.

Since that day, I have come to understand how some of the characters in the Bible were able to react and respond as they did when they encountered angels. I often used to wonder how I would have responded if I was Mary, the mother of Jesus. We read the story of Mary's encounter with the angel Gabriel in Luke 1:26–38. Mary was just a young girl when he appeared and told her she was going to have a baby. Her response was not fear, just confusion about how this was going to come about. The angel quietly explained that the Holy Spirit would overshadow her and she would become pregnant. She was blessed and highly favoured. I wondered how Mary managed to respond as she did: so calm and accepting, "Let it be to me according to your word" (NKJV). How did she know this being was an angel? Was it the huge wings that gave him away or was it his smooth talking? No, she just knew. I understand now that this experience brought her into the Lord's presence. She understood what she would never be able to explain in words – that God is God and that with Him, all things are possible.

The Lord understood only too well that she would never be able to communicate this news to Joseph, her young fiancé. However, he also had a visit from an angel as he slept. We read the account in Matthew 1:18–24. Joseph had been considering breaking off his engagement to Mary when he found out that she was pregnant. He was understandably confused but the angel began by telling him not to be afraid. Joseph knew when he woke up that he had had a real encounter. This was not just any old dream, he had met his Lord through the visiting angel and somehow he knew that everything was going to be all right.

The encounters Mary and Joseph had with the angels gave them the courage, the strength, and the ability to walk through the rest of their lives, which included the death, as a young man, of their son Jesus. The Father knew the kind of strength they were going to need to parent Jesus, but also that unlike any other normal boy, He wouldn't be theirs to keep. This was God's Son.

I believe that there are times in all our lives when we find ourselves in places where we do not know how to pray any more. There are times when things happen that cause us to cry out for a fresh revelation of Jesus. Times when we don't just want to hear about what Jesus can do: we need to see it for ourselves. It has been my experience over the years that this occurs exactly when I am going through the most difficult challenges, and the more pressure I experience, the more this pushes me to reach out to God in ways I don't when life is going along nicely. I believe this is true for all of us. It is only when we come to the end of what is possible for us that God can step in and do the impossible. The reality is, we don't need God for things that are possible.

I have a firm belief that there are angels all around. I know that God is able to open our eyes to see into another dimension where angels dwell but that somehow He first has to permeate *our* hearts and bring *us* to a place of deep longing to know Him better. It is a place where He can trust us with what He puts into our hearts; our hearts live for His glory. He will not ever give His glory to another but He draws us into His presence so we can have fellowship with Him and so that He can reveal His deep and mysterious ways to us. He is our Father and we are His children.

The night the angels came for me was a first. As I talked to David afterwards, he just smiled casually as he told me that angels were frequent visitors to him and had even become the norm when he got up to pray in the middle of the night. He talked about sometimes not actually seeing anything but yet being aware of a beautiful aroma. If he saw something like a rainbow, it was accompanied by heavenly music. As he talked and I listened, I found myself wanting to know and experience so much more.

Over time, just as when those angels visited David and me that evening, I have also been challenged and provoked to reach deeper into God having witnessed the Holy Spirit at work in some of the lives of my brothers and sisters in Africa. It seems to me that the Father wants to reveal so much to us as we open our hearts and our lives to Him. Most of us do not see angels on a regular basis but Jesus can, and does, reveal Himself through other people. I have seen the Holy Spirit at work in the lives of some of my brothers and sisters in Africa in a way that has challenged and provoked me to reach deeper into God in the same way as when the angels visited. The Holy Spirit can provoke us to be better, kinder, more loving, more understanding, and more compassionate: provoked to be more like Jesus.

As we came to the end of our time at the healing centre, I could not have imagined the turn of events that was about to take place. One thing I was sure of, Jesus was in complete control. He had me right where He wanted me and doing what He had prepared and called me to do.

I believe that God opened my eyes to see those angels, not just to make me feel safe and secure, but because that whole encounter equipped, prepared, and carried me through a diabolically brutal civil war.

CHAPTER 3

THE FIRST WAR BABY ARRIVES

When we arrived in the city I went to stay with my friends John and Penny who had been looking after Hannah and Lydia after their evacuation a couple of weeks earlier. It soon became very clear that the unrest in the country was not going to disappear overnight and that we were not going to return to normality any time soon.

I managed to rent a small two-bedroom house in the city. Once we were settled there, the staff from the clinic and I started to help at one of the camps that had been set up about 2 km away. This camp provided refuge for about 2,000 displaced people. Camps had sprung up everywhere to assist those who had fled from the fighting in the mountains to the relative safety of the city. Many public buildings were also teeming with displaced folk: desperate people whose homes had been destroyed and family members slaughtered.

One Sunday morning, one of the nurses from my clinic who was working at this camp, arrived at my home with the pastor from the church, along with a five-day-old baby.

He was accompanied by the baby's father and one of his brothers. They came inside and asked me if I would take this little boy and be his mother. His own mother had died during childbirth and his father felt he would have a better chance of survival if I took him. As I held him in my arms, my heart felt like it was going to burst with excitement because this was the baby I had dreamed about a year ago – before he had even been born. This was the baby boy I had been waiting for and talking about for months.

When I picked him up and felt his breath on my neck, it was as if I was back in that dream I had experienced. I knew that this was the baby in that dream. I couldn't help but recall verses 13–16 in Psalm 139:

> *You made all the delicate, inner parts of my body and knit me together in my mother's womb. Thank you for making me so wonderfully complex! Your workmanship is marvellous – how well I know it. You watched me as I was being formed in utter seclusion, as I was woven together in the dark of the womb. You saw me before I was born. Every day of my life was recorded in your book. Every moment was laid out before a single day had passed.*

It was another amazing "God moment" as I held this little bundle in my arms with his mass of soft, curly hair. I had been aware of his birth a few days prior to his arrival at my home. My friend Sarah had heard on the grapevine that a baby had been born and tragically the mother had died after the delivery. The baby's father had five other children (one of them being a physically disabled toddler), and had sought refuge in the camp where we were helping out.

After the birth, an old lady who was a family friend, had stayed at the hospital with the baby as his father had no way to feed or look after him. He was looking for someone to take care of his child. He made enquiries and found a Russian lady who was married to a Burundian man who had been looking for a baby to adopt. This Russian lady went straight to the hospital to see the baby. Strangely, she was informed by the old lady that the baby was a girl! This prospective adopted mother took the baby and asked for a blood test and a medical examination before committing to take the baby home. Then, to their great surprise, when this baby was undressed for a medical, she was found to be a he: it was a baby boy! This was not too much of a problem for the couple. Two days passed while they waited for the blood test results which all came back normal. The baby was found to be in good health. There was a subsequent conversation with the child's father. This couple, keen to adopt the baby, were very clear that if his father gave him up to them, they would never want him to have any contact with them again. They were clear that they would raise him as their own but the child would never be able to see his father or his family again. Understandably, for a man still in deep grief from losing his wife, he simply refused to give his son to this couple. The deal was off. He took his baby son and went back to the camp.

Another two days passed and it was at this point that I got the phone call from the nurse in the camp telling me about this baby who had only been drinking water and black tea from a spoon since he was born and, now at five days old, was not doing well. They asked if I could help. Of course I could! As this baby was handed to me, his father asked me if I would be his mother so that he could live. I told him about my dream and that this was the little boy I had carried in my heart even before he was conceived. I felt God had told me to give him the name Benjamin (meaning son of my right hand), and Benjamin it is.

Many years have passed and right now Benjamin is nearly twenty-two. His father, brothers, and sisters still keep in touch and he sees them from time to time. Now studying at a university in England, Benjamin was the first baby to arrive at my house after the war started. At that point I had no thoughts or plans to collect any more babies as I had my two girls and now my son. I would keep helping out where I was needed and try and work out how all four of us were going to manage when I went back to my one-bedroom mud house on the mountain; just a matter of time I again mistakenly thought.

While I was getting myself organized in my new two-bedroom house, big enough for us for now, two young men began to work for me at home. One of them was Deo, who had worked for me at the clinic helping to guard the premises and also sterilizing my instruments in a pressure cooker. I discovered Deo knew how to cook so now I had a house boy/cook. Alexi became a night guard for us (he had previously had this role at the healing centre) and also did a bit of gardening in the mornings. Now all I needed was a house girl who would be able to help me with some cleaning and laundry and to look after the children when I worked in the camp.

By now it was early February 1994. Lydia was almost five and needed to be registered at a new school nearer to where we now lived. Hannah was fourteen months old and Benjamin a newborn. Once again my friend Sarah came to the rescue. Within the English-speaking community church there were many families from other surrounding African countries who were working in Burundi, but at that time, because of the escalation in fighting, many companies and organizations, including schools and banks, were closing down. Dozens of expatriates subsequently started to leave the country to get repatriated in their own countries. Sarah knew a couple who were leaving and who had a young house girl who could speak a little English (this came to be a big help as my Kirundi still left a lot to be desired!). This eighteen-year-old with a winning smile came to see me one morning; her name was Gaudiose. The children she had been looking after in her previous job could not pronounce her name so she became known as Rosa. She seemed quite mature for her age and could thankfully understand quite a lot of what I was saying. Her understanding of my English was rather better than my understanding of her English when we talked. With two babies in nappies needing a lot of attention and frequent feeding, we quickly agreed a salary. I now had all the help I needed and finally managed to get into some kind of routine.

At that time I was visiting the various camps for displaced people for a few hours at a time when I could. The situation was overwhelming, with so many desperate people and so much need. There were many women and children there who had fled their homes with only a few belongings. No one had escaped without losing friends, loved ones, or family members. The camps were basically huge fields with no buildings and certainly no kind of sanitation or running water. Burundians are mainly farmers who live off their crops and buy and sell in local markets. The women are used to working in the fields tending their crops all day, with their babies strapped to their backs and their toddlers at their feet. Generally they live as extended families in community and look after each other. The children learn from their mothers and grandmothers how to plant crops, carry water, and cook. From about the age of six or seven, girls are often seen with their baby brothers and sisters strapped to their backs and are taught from a very early age how to survive. Now, here they were in the camp with nothing: no food or water and no idea how they were going to survive such conditions.

The aid agencies were working non-stop to try and distribute plastic sheeting for makeshift tents. Others were trying to give out food and clean water but there was so much chaos and fear causing people to panic that the situation in the camps was far from organized. One thing that became very clear to me very early on when I started working in one particular camp was that young children who did not have a mother or a mother figure to look after them simply got lost in the crowd. Some of the children – some as young as eighteen months old – had been picked up and rescued by people fleeing from the fighting. People would just grab an abandoned child and run with it to save its life. Once in the camp, no one could take on the responsibility for someone else's baby or child so they often got left in a corner somewhere. Very young children who had seen the most terrible acts of violence became completely traumatized. We would find them sitting motionless, staring into space with empty eyes, looking like hopeless old men and women in babies' bodies.

These camps were filled with the badly injured and of course, with the lack of sanitation and clean water, typhoid and cholera hit hard. Only the strongest survived. The biggest challenge for me at that point was how I could possibly help some of the babies and traumatized children: they had no one to stand in line with them for the cup of porridge that was being handed out. They were simply overlooked and forgotten. The babies had no milk formula because it was too expensive and even if we could get hold of some, there was frustratingly no clean water to make it up or means of sterilizing a bottle. This was an absolute nightmare. I had never felt so desperate or helpless. Where were my angels now? I began to dread going to that camp.

I was so challenged by the overwhelming need. We did what we could with what we had in handing out a few supplies of medicines and what food we could get hold of. However, over a period of a few weeks, I became desperate to try and do something more. I just needed to know what and how.

By April of that year, the camps were getting slightly more organized as other agencies were now involved and things began to feel a little less tense, although there was still a lot of heavy gunfire and the fighting continued day and night. On one April night in particular it was as if all hell broke loose. The word came that once again Burundi's second newly elected president, together with Rwanda's president, had been killed. They were in a plane together that was shot down out of the sky. What followed was the massive genocide in Rwanda. It was estimated that over a million people were killed over a very short period of time. The countries of Burundi and Rwanda are separated only by a man-made border. It was just a matter of days before people started to flee over the border into Burundi to escape. It seemed to me at the time a bit like jumping out of a frying pan, straight into another fire.

Within days of the war starting in Rwanda, literally dozens of expatriate families who had stuck it out and stayed in Burundi, hoping and praying that the situation would settle, now started to leave. Every day more and more people left. Daily, the flights coming in were empty but were leaving full to bursting. Dozens of houses that had been rented now lay empty with no new tenants around to rent them. It was a horrendous situation for the local people and particularly for the house-owners who relied on those rents to pay for their livelihood.

One afternoon in May, when Benjamin was four months old, I decided to take him for a short walk in his pram. I had seventeen-month-old Hannah sitting on the other end, and Lydia walking at the side. As we walked past a row of very large houses, a lady came out of the gate of one of them. I recognized her vaguely as she used to go to the English-speaking church from time to time. She told me that she and her family were leaving and suggested to me that I talk to the landlord of the house. She thought that a lower rent was more acceptable to the landlord than no rent at all and that it was better to have people renting and looking after the house than leaving it empty. I became quite excited at her suggestion but then more than a little daunted when she told me they were paying US $1,200 a month to rent this spacious five-bedroom home. I was just about managing to pay the $250 a month for my little two-bedroom duplex. I asked to look around the lovely grounds. It had a huge garden with luscious fruit trees. A large mango tree caught my eye and then, when I turned and saw the avocado tree, I knew I was interested! I went inside the house and immediately felt such peace that God was going to make a way for me to move into this house. Not only did it have those five bedrooms, it also had a wonderful large airy sitting room. I started to picture maybe adopting another two or three babies and helping many more people.

I didn't get any further on our afternoon walk. I took the name and the phone number of the landlord and when I got home, the first thing I did was ring round the few friends who were still in Burundi. I explained about the house and that I felt God prompting me to go for it. I asked them to pray that the rent would be acceptable and that I would be able to afford it. I did not tell them that the $250 a month I was currently paying was just about all I could afford. We prayed and I managed to get an appointment with the landlord. He spoke English, which was a big help. He was quite taken with my three children and very open to renting the house to me and lowering the rent. I explained that I wasn't working for a big aid agency who gave substantial rent allowances and that all I could offer was $400. I felt that even though I had no idea at that moment how I was going to pay it, $400 was what I should offer.

After a lot of discussion, I began to say that I was sorry for wasting his time because I just didn't have any more to offer, but he suddenly stopped and agreed! Having said yes he went away to draw up a one-year contract for $400 a month. To say I was astonished would be a complete understatement. I was in shock. I was excited because I knew God was in this but was also in quite a dilemma because I didn't know at that moment how I was going to pay! Later in the evening, I phoned around my friends to let them know I had got the house. To my great surprise, one of those calls left me in yet another state of sheer amazement. One friend who worked for an organization that helped children in need decided to contact her boss and explain that I was also trying to help vulnerable children. She asked if there was any way they could help me by contributing towards rent on a new house. She had just heard back from them that they would commit to $400 a month for a year – the exact amount I needed to cover all the rent!

I often wonder why we are so amazed when God shows up in the most unexpected ways. It makes me wonder how much more we would see and experience if we lived life full of expectation. One of the greatest challenges to me comes in Luke 18:8: "when the Son of Man returns, how many will he find on the earth who have faith?" I have discovered – and am still discovering – that when I live with the expectation of experiencing God at work in my life and through the lives of others, I am rarely disappointed. I just have to look with the eyes of faith and have an expectant attitude.

At this point I had been in Burundi almost four years. In many ways it felt like a lifetime. I could not imagine being back in England and knew that after my experiences over the last six months my life would never be the same again. I longed to see the power of the Holy Spirit as described in the Scriptures; to see the same power that raised Christ from the dead dwelling in me to quicken my mortal body. I felt completely helpless and totally out of my depth in the middle of such massive challenges and such acute need. In all honesty I felt the vulnerability of being one of the few expatriates left in the country. I didn't have any deep desire to leave and did not feel afraid, but sometimes I felt slightly trapped because having the children meant I couldn't leave Burundi. Once again the Lord prompted me to start processing documents for the children and in the meantime to apply for passports for them so that I would be able to take them with me if and when I travelled. Again, it was a miracle as God seemed to give us favour in every office with every document for all three children. I managed to get passports and visas for them to visit the UK relatively easily.

Finally, in June 1994, we moved into our lovely new five-bedroom house. Everyone was in one room: Ben in a crib; the girls in bunk beds; and Rosa, our new nanny, on another bunk bed – quite a luxury for her as in our previous house, dear Rosa had had to make do sleeping on a mattress on the kitchen floor with the hum of an ancient and noisy fridge to lull her to sleep at night! We had certainly come up in the world from mud hut to palatial dwelling in a very short period of time. We spent about a week unpacking and sorting things out. I then took all three children for a six-week break in the UK.

We left on a flight with some friends who were going back to live in the UK. This was a great help as travelling with two babies and a five-year-old was not easy. Rosa stayed behind to keep house while we were gone. Jean Cordle, a dear friend from our home church in Cheam in Surrey offered us accommodation. We packed into her small home. It was cosy and so good to drop off to sleep without the sound of gunfire.

It was a strange feeling to be back in the UK. At that time many people were talking about a new outpouring of the Holy Spirit. They called it the "Toronto Blessing". It seemed a church in Toronto, Canada, was experiencing a supernatural outpouring of the Holy Spirit and many people were travelling from all over the world to this church to experience something new. We heard they were having meetings every day and evening – inviting the Lord to visit them and touch them afresh. Just as we arrived at my home church in Cheam, meetings were also being planned for every evening, with the expectation that God would move by His Spirit in their hungry hearts. I certainly felt the need to be refilled and ministered to afresh and looked forward to anything God wanted to do that might equip me for whatever I would need to face back in Burundi. I was ready. Every night after tea I got the children bathed and into their pyjamas, and at 7.30 p.m., off to church – just a ten-minute walk – complete with sleeping bags for the girls to curl up in at the back of the meeting hall and a bottle for Ben if and when needed. This was our routine night after night for six weeks.

All around people laughed, cried, fell down, and got up feeling different and refreshed. Some would shake: all manner of people experiencing all manner of different things. In fact, one evening Lydia asked me, "Mummy, are we going to the laughing meeting tonight?" It was an amazing time but also very frustrating for me as each night

I turned up saying to myself and to the Lord, "This is my night. Tonight, something is going to happen to me," and night after night I stood like a stick of rock, hands in the air, heart and arms open, expecting something. Everyone around me either laughing, crying, or falling down on the floor like drunken people – but for me, nothing. Absolutely nothing, time and time again. I just did not understand what was wrong with me. Too soon it was time for me to fly back to Burundi, excited that God was taking me back for a purpose but also with quite a deep disappointment that I had not seemed to experience anything like the other folk around me in this new move of the Spirit.

It wasn't until we touched down in Burundi the next morning that I had the experience I had been waiting for. I was filled with the most amazing sense of God's presence. I had such a deep sense of purpose that God was with me and that He had a plan for my life. I became aware that He was calling me into a new season. I felt my heart being filled with a new depth of purpose and with it came a fresh infilling of His grace and wisdom and love. Every night, for six weeks, I had sat in meetings feeling nothing, but within ten minutes of touching down in Burundi, it was like God poured into me everything I needed for that moment and indeed for the months to come. That was a lesson. Never underestimate what God is doing. Feelings come and go but God knows us so well. He knows how to reach us. He knows exactly what we need and when we need to feel His presence. God is God. He knows what's best.

It was so good to see Rosa again. Deo had managed to get a big sheet of waterproof covering to keep the rain out of his outdoor kitchen. It was time to get settled again and to see what this next season held for us. I have often taken time to pause and look back at the way God has led me. In His great wisdom He does not show the whole picture of what is ahead but little by little, one step at a time, His plan for our lives unfolds and it is our job to walk in obedience to what He shows us.

I originally came to Burundi because of a connection through Roffey Place Christian Training Centre I had attended in England for a year in 1985. I didn't actually want to go to that particular Bible school, but one in America. I did my best to push as hard as I could to get to the US, but my church leaders didn't feel that it was right. In the end, through gritted teeth, I followed the wise advice of those in leadership who knew me well and ended up at Roffey Place.

In fact, this is where I first heard about Burundi. It was Bob Gordon, the director of Roffey Place, who brought me to Burundi for two weeks as part of a small team praying for the sick while Bob was teaching and preaching in the country. When we returned to the UK I decided to stay on at the college and work with Bob as part of his ministry team there before eventually going to Burundi again for what I thought would be two years.

"What if?" has been a question that has caused me to thank God for stopping me make the wrong decision. What if I hadn't gone to that training centre? I never would have gone to Burundi and never would have connected with my children and all the people who have come to Burundi to help me with the work that God called me to do. Some of these people met and married their lifelong partners in Burundi. Of course, it's all hypothetical because I did get to Burundi, but it never ceases to amaze me that God's plan for each one of us is that we make a difference in this world. Wherever we are, whatever work we are involved in, God's plan for every one of us is that we will make a difference in the lives of those He connects us with. The deep cry from my heart as I was asking the Lord for guidance was that He would give me such clarity to know what I should be doing next. Who were the people I was supposed to be helping and connecting with? It was not good enough to just set off aimlessly into the camps without such clarity. The needs of crowds of people were overwhelming and it was futile to even think I could help anyone after being away for six weeks. I knew the numbers in the camps would have swelled because of the overflow of many people from Rwanda and also because of the ongoing war in Burundi. There were very few people left who I could team up with to go and help. The nurses who had worked with me had now left the country and made their way back to their own countries of Kenya and Uganda. This was not a time to do my own thing.

I prayed and asked God to show me clearly what His plan was for me and to connect me with others that I could work with. My language skills were still pretty basic and to be of any help I felt I needed to be able to communicate. It was also quite dangerous and extremely emotionally draining to be working alone. However, once again, God gave me clear direction and he led me to join with a couple of American missionaries who had been in Burundi for a while and who had planted a small church. They were helping out with a team of local people from their church. It was fantastic to have someone to talk to and pray with as we looked to the Lord for guidance, wisdom, and provision to help in the camp we felt drawn to work in – the first camp I had started in – the camp where Benjamin's family were still living.

It was now almost a year since the war started and still there seemed to be no sign of it ever ending. Even when the fighting eventually stopped, and it had to sometime, where were all these displaced people going to go? What were they going to do? There was nothing to go back to. All their homes had been destroyed. The whole country was a picture of absolute desolation and carnage. Here we were again, in that familiar position of needing such wisdom to know what to do and what to say to people who were rapidly losing all hope. It is a fact that people can live without food for quite a long time. You can even live without water for a few days. But people do not survive without hope. Our challenge was how to lead them to Him – the one who promises to provide for all of their needs and gives hope to the hopeless.

CHAPTER 4

HOW I FOUND GOD IN THE MIDDLE OF THIS MESS

Each morning would begin with a group of us going into the camp, which was overflowing with desperate, displaced people. We would take *ubuyi* (porridge made of maize ground into flour) in vast quantities to feed the children. We would pour it into large dustbins and put it onto the back of a truck and transport it down into the camp. All the young children who could stand in a line with a cup were fed and we concentrated on those under five years of age. Breastfeeding and pregnant women were also prioritized.

One morning we went through our usual routine of handing out the cups of *ubuyi* to these children. When we came to the end of the line, we starting clearing up and I discovered a little bit of food left in the bottom of one of the bins. I started looking around and saw a very old man sitting cross-legged in the dirt. I felt there was something about him. He was holding an empty cup and seemed to be praying. My friend and I went to sit with him to find out his story. As my Kirundi wasn't very good my friend helped interpret for me. The old man, stooped down with age and suffering, proceeded to tell us his story.

He said he was eighty-four years of age and had walked from an area up in the mountains – about 20 km away; it had taken him over five days to reach the camp. He tearfully told us his wife and all his five children and their families had been killed and his house had been destroyed. He had somehow miraculously escaped. He had lost everything – all he had were the clothes on his back. I went and scraped the bottom of the bin to give him a cup of *ubuyi*. As I handed this to him, he looked at me and said, "Madam missionary, I never realized that Jesus was all I needed, until Jesus was all I had."

At that moment, it struck me that this old man's God was so much bigger than my God. I was provoked that day and have been ever since to ask myself how big my God is. I stood in that camp day after day and asked myself the question, "How do you find God in the middle of all this mess?"

Over the years I have had the opportunity to travel to and speak in churches and Christian gatherings in the UK and across Canada and America. I have shared this man's testimony and years later his words still have the same powerful impact on people. For me, to meet someone still so in love with Jesus in these dire circumstances made me stop and wonder for a moment if I was even saved. Such was the impact his words had. It is not that difficult to love

Jesus and to sing His praises when everything is going well. However, how do we react when our whole world feels like it has come to a complete standstill?

There are many stories in the Bible of people overcoming the most horrendous circumstances but somehow, when we read, we can stay detached because we think those people are not like us and the events occurred long ago. But after meeting this old man, I found myself able to identify with the apostle Paul in the New Testament. He talked about how he had learned to be content in every situation. In Philippians 4:11–13, he says:

> *for I have learned how to be content with whatever I have. I know how to live on almost nothing or with everything. I have learned the secret of living in every situation, whether it is with a full stomach or empty, with plenty or little. For I can do everything through Christ, who gives me strength.*

Also, in 1 Thessalonians 5:18 Paul says, "Be thankful in all circumstances, for this is God's will for you who belong to Christ Jesus."

The challenge the apostle Paul and this old man I met set before us is this: How big is your God? These men discovered a secret: the secret of experiencing absolute contentment in every situation. They somehow managed to embrace the vastness of God and to stand in the middle of devastating circumstances because the God they knew, trusted, and loved was so much bigger than any situation that can be endured on earth. Again, Paul, in 2 Corinthians 4:17 (NIV) says "For our light and momentary troubles are achieving for us an eternal glory that far outweighs them all." In other words, there is nothing we can go through that is anything more than a light and momentary trouble. The only way we can ever try to understand or comprehend this truth is to get a glimpse of eternity: to be able to walk through the kinds of trials and tribulations that the Corinthians were experiencing and still be able to give thanks. They were given a glimpse, a revelation, of the bigger picture and a deep assurance that they were here, passing through this life, for just a short time. Eternity is our ultimate destination. With this comes an assurance that God is so much bigger than anything we could ever experience.

Jesus never promised to take us out of problems but he does promise to take us through. In Psalm 23:4 we read, "though I walk through the valley of the shadow of death, I will fear no evil; For You are with me; Your rod and Your staff, they comfort me" (NKJV). God is in the valley. To know Jesus is to know that death is only a shadow. There is eternity beyond. For this old man, he knew without a shadow of a doubt that he would be with his Jesus and also reunited with his family who also loved Jesus. There were tears of grief but no sting of death for these folk. Jesus was their Lord eternally; eternity was their final destination.

It was not long before my feelings of dread in going to that camp every day turned to feelings of expectancy and at times an incomprehensible excitement (humanly speaking). It seemed this old man was not unique in his discovery of the mighty God and I found myself time after time being so blessed and encouraged by the people I was trying to help.

One day, I was asked if I would help out with a vaccination programme for the children. Starting this programme felt a bit like locking the door after the horse had bolted, as measles unfortunately had already broken out in the camp. Sure enough, several days passed and dozens of children were showing symptoms. In such close confinement, with almost 3,000 people in the camp, hundreds of children were affected. Of course, measles is usually quite harmless, but in the heat of Africa, babies and little ones under two years of age who had high fevers and who were already weakened from malnutrition, succumbed to the disease. Dozens of these little children died. Now, faced with more challenges of finding money for burials, the grief of those families was once again overwhelming. Still, so many of them were giving thanks and encouraging each other that there was a place they could find refuge and healing in the shadow of His wings. Psalm 91:1–2 became such a reality in that camp: "Those who live in the shelter of the Most High, will find rest in the shadow of the Almighty. This I declare about the Lord: He alone is my refuge, my place of safety; he is my God, and I trust Him." This they were doing, day after day.

One morning I was drawn to the sound of singing in one corner of the field where some of the mothers had gathered. There was a lady among them whose baby had tragically just died. She had wrapped her child in a colourful *Ibitenge* (bright African cotton) and she had carefully laid him at her feet waiting for the funeral. She stood with these other women, forming a circle, and a man with a stick seemed to be conducting them. They were singing an old hymn in Kirundi, with hands lifted high in praise to God, eyes looking up to heaven, and tears rolling down their faces. Right in the midst of the fetid smells of cholera, typhoid, and human decay, the scene seemed to display such apparent hopelessness but their voices rang out with such conviction:

> *When peace, like a river, attendeth my way,*
> *When sorrows like sea billows roll;*
> *Whatever my lot, Thou hast taught me to say,*
> *It is well, it is well with my soul.*
>
> *Though Satan should buffet, though trials should come,*
> *Let this blest assurance control,*
> *That Christ hath regarded my helpless estate,*
> *And hath shed His own blood for my soul.*
>
> *It is well with my soul,*
> *It is well, it is well with my soul.*
>
> *My sin – oh, the bliss of this glorious thought! –*
> *My sin, not in part but the whole,*
> *Is nailed to the cross, and I bear it no more,*
> *Praise the Lord, praise the Lord, O my soul!*

It is well with my soul,
It is well, it is well with my soul.

For me, be it Christ, be it Christ hence to live:
If Jordan above me shall roll,
No pang shall be mine, for in death as in life
Thou wilt whisper Thy peace to my soul.

It is well with my soul,
It is well, it is well with my soul.

But, Lord, 'tis for Thee, for Thy coming we wait,
The sky, not the grave, is our goal;
Oh trump of the angel! Oh voice of the Lord!
Blessèd hope, blessèd rest of my soul!

It is well with my soul,
It is well, it is well with my soul.

And Lord, haste the day when my faith shall be sight,
The clouds be rolled back as a scroll;
The trump shall resound, and the Lord shall descend,
Even so, it is well with my soul.

It is well with my soul,
It is well, it is well with my soul.

This hymn was written in 1873 by Horatio G. Spafford. He was a successful lawyer with a wife and five children. But a series of personal tragedies struck: in 1870 his only son had died of scarlet fever, and a year later the great Chicago fire consumed Spafford's real estate investments. He lost his entire life savings. Then, in 1873, Spafford and his family decided to take a vacation to Europe. But Spafford was delayed by last-minute business. He sent his wife and four daughters on the *Ville du Havre* and promised to follow in a few days' time. On 22 November the ship was struck by an iron sailing vessel and it sank in twelve minutes. A total of 226 people were killed, including Spafford's four daughters. When the survivors of the shipwreck landed in Europe, Anna Spafford cabled her husband. "Saved alone. What shall I do?" Spafford immediately left Chicago to bring his wife home. In the midst of his sorrow while sailing near the site of his beloved daughters' deaths, he wrote the words of this hymn. Here we find someone else who over 100 years ago discovered that God is bigger than their circumstances, and who chose Jesus in the depth of his grief.

In the midst of a refugee camp in Third World Africa, Spafford's words lived on to bless, encourage, lift the hearts, and give hope to others: the message was that there is so much more for them to experience than what they are enduring now.

There is a desperation for Jesus that comes at times of deep pain: a desperation that pushes us into God in ways that are impossible when things are going well. I do not believe that it is God's plan that only those who suffer great loss and bereavement are able to experience the love, peace, and power of God as these men and women did, but it seems clear that there needs to be a deep hunger after

God – a desperate need for more of Him. The challenge is: how hungry for God are we? The deeper the pit we find ourselves in and the more intense the pressure, the more desperate we become, and it is in this depth of desperation that we reach out to God. As we reach out, the wonderful revelation dawns on us that all we need to do is press on, to take hold of that for which Christ Jesus took hold of us (Philippians 3:12). It is in the pressing on that we become those who overcome: we live in the reality of knowing that what God does in us, He will do *through* us. His desire is to show us His faithfulness so that we can become vessels and carriers of His faithfulness, love, and grace: we are carriers of Jesus that we might *become* Jesus to those we struggle to help, those we are longing to introduce to our Saviour and Lord. And in this we become carriers of Jesus.

***

One afternoon a seventeen-year-old girl turned up at my house. She looked like so many of the young people who were in the camps: rather unkempt, thin, and traumatized. Her huge dark eyes looked like the eyes of someone much older who has seen a lifetime of suffering. The look was shocking and heartbreaking. We sat this young girl down and gave her some food and water and prepared to hear her story.

She had fled from Rwanda, walking and hitching lifts. She told us that one night the village where she lived with her family was attacked. Two of her siblings had fled. She managed to climb up into a space in the roof and hide. She watched as her parents and several other family members were killed by two men wielding machetes. She sat very still for what seemed like hours and then the attackers started to move around all the houses in the compound and dragged outside all the dead bodies of the people they had killed. One by one they began to set alight the houses and to burn them down. Realizing she couldn't stay hidden in the roof now, this young girl sneaked outside into the courtyard and hid, burying herself under the dead bodies of her own family. She was not sure how long she stayed hidden there but remembered it going dark twice while she lay unseen. Eventually thirst gave her enough courage to move. She was far too exhausted and traumatized to give an account or to remember how she escaped, and seemed to have no idea how she arrived at my house.

There were many similar stories as the weeks passed. I met another lady one day in the camp. She was giving a testimony to another group about how she had stayed hiding for several weeks in a small derelict house after her family had been killed. She told them that just outside the place where she was hiding, there was a small patch of garden. She had been praying and asking God to provide food for her in her famished and weakened state. She knew that with no food or water she would not survive very long. One morning, just as it was getting light, she noticed some mushrooms growing in the garden. She slowly and quietly slipped out from where she was hiding, picked the mushrooms, and found an empty milk can that just happened to be half-full of rain water. "Breakfast and lunch – what an amazing answer to prayer," she thought. Can you imagine how she felt when the next morning she peered through the crack in the door and once again there were fresh mushrooms on the lawn? For five weeks she dined on these heavenly mushrooms that appeared every morning.

Some people told of how, against the odds, when the attackers came, it was as if they became invisible, hidden from the enemy. It was an amazing thing to witness as small groups would gather together to sing and pray and give thanks that their lives had been spared, and to hear testimonies of how God had helped them. Some told of how God provided for them from strangers who just seemed to appear and were never seen again. Others talked about how God's healing was released as they cried out, "Teach us, Lord, show us how to forgive so that on that wonderful day when we meet You, we will also be forgiven. Teach us Lord, how to forgive." The Lord did, in His own time and His own way.

One Sunday morning, in the middle of a church service, a lady came staggering to the front of the church. She had a bucket of water in her hands. She made her way over to two young men who were sitting in the congregation. She took off their socks and shoes and began to wash their feet. When she finished, she addressed the congregation. She explained how several months ago some men who were of the opposite ethnic group to her broke into her home and killed her two sons. She had not been able to forgive these men and felt such deep anger and bitterness that she had no peace. She felt her relationship with God was dying because of this. That morning, God directed her to these two young men. They were not the men guilty of killing her sons but they were the same ethnic group as the perpetrators. She was choosing to forgive. As she gave this testimony, it was as if the Holy Spirit descended on the meeting. All over the congregation people began crying and screaming. That morning, God did what no one else could do. In one hour, literally hundreds of people were delivered and set free from unforgiveness. On that morning, because of the obedience of one woman, people who had not experienced peace or joy for months went home set free from bitterness. It became common to hear testimonies of miraculous healings. God was at work in the middle of this mess.

Another time, I found myself meditating on a story from Mark 2:1–5. This describes the time that Jesus was in a house ministering and praying for people. There were crowds of people inside and out. Four friends carried a paralysed man on a mat but there were so many people that they just couldn't find a way through them to get him to Jesus. We don't know how far they had carried him. We don't know how many hours it had taken them to get there, but we do know by the actions of what they did next that they were desperate and determined they were not going to carry this man back home again. They found a way to get up on the roof and proceeded to dig a hole through the clay that was big enough for their friend to fit through and be lowered down to where Jesus was, and that was that. I imagine when he got healed, he ran home! The thing that strikes me when I read this is that there was no doubt in the minds of those men that Jesus was going to heal their friend. They just had to find a way to get to Him.

People ask me time and time again why we hear so many stories of amazing miracles, transforming deliverances, and healings happening in the Third World. Accounts we hear about people being raised from the dead often come from Africa, India, or other poverty-stricken places. I think the answer is so clear – it is because these people are desperate. Often there are no hospitals or doctors so Jesus has to be their first choice. In the West, where doctors are readily available and there is a heavy reliance on medicine being able to cure many ills, Jesus becomes our second or even our last choice when things don't go according to plan. When we find that doctors can't help us, it is only then we turn in desperation to Jesus. It is very common in Africa on Sunday mornings to find people sitting around the perimeter of the church as 10–12,000 people meet to worship God. There are those who have walked for several hours with their sick relatives and friends. Mothers come with their children along with the deaf, the blind, and even the dying. They sit and wait until the end of the service, which can last four or five hours, in the hot and humid African climate. Then they make their way forward for prayer. They are desperate. They have no money for doctors or hospitals. There are no social services in the Third World, so they come and believe and are determined that they will not go home until Jesus has healed them. Week after week, Jesus heals them. They are certain that Jesus will heal them; He is their first port of call. Blind eyes are open, deaf ears begin to hear, the sick are healed, and the captives are set free as the name of Jesus is spoken over them. Not all get healed every time, but prayer does not stop because some don't experience a miracle that day. Some return week after week believing and trusting that one day Jesus will pass their way, never staying away in case they miss their moment. It is without doubt one of the most humbling experiences to witness. They certainly would not exchange that for any amount of money in the world – the touch of Jesus is priceless.

Just at the side of the church meeting place at the centre of the city, there is a small hospital that is run by the Christian mission I work with. There is a small maternity clinic in this hospital and one day we heard how a lady had given birth to a baby who was born dead. It had been a long and difficult delivery and all attempts to revive the baby boy had failed. He was washed and wrapped up in a large sheet and left in the delivery room while arrangements were made to take his little body for burial. A whole night passed. The next morning, the cleaning lady who happened to be a Christian, heard about the baby and went into the delivery room, picked the child up, and proceeded to march around the delivery room and then out into the hospital grounds crying out to God for His life – praying and speaking over him that God's promises for him were for life and not for death, for good and not for evil. After a while, the sheet was opened, the baby was alive –Jesus had raised him from the dead! He seemed to have suffered no ill effects from this ordeal. His mother named him Lazarus and the family went home overjoyed, to share what Jesus had done for them with anyone they passed on their way.

During this period of terrible conflict, it felt as if there was a blanket of grief over the whole country. Not one family had escaped the devastating effects of the war. However, there was a tangible change in mood and atmosphere in the camps as many people renewed their trust in God and could identify with the words in Philippians 3:13–14:

> *I focus on this one thing: Forgetting the past and looking forward to what lies ahead, I press on to reach the end of the race and receive the heavenly prize for which God, through Jesus Christ, is calling us.*

Going into the camps was like entering another world. It was a bit like riding a roller coaster: some days everyone I talked to seemed to be coping well. Other days, when there had been a new influx of people, a deep depression seemed to consume everyone. Added to this, it was not always easy to travel back and forth from my home. Some days we would set out only to discover that our road was completely blocked by groups of men who were causing as much disruption as they could by aiming to stop the movement of cars into the city. There were gangs of thieves around who played on people's fear, and on a regular basis we found intruders trying to get into our compound at night.

One evening I was invited to go to some friends for dinner. They lived a couple of miles away on the other side of the town. I didn't really like going out at night but I thought for this once, it would be OK. The girls were in bed and sleeping and Benjamin was a little bit restless so I decided to take him with me. I took him in his basket and put him in the back of my Land Cruiser. However, it was not long before I realized I had made a big mistake! Instead of sticking to the main road, I decided to take a short cut down a dirt track. After about 200 yards, I saw a group of people standing by a car and two people on the floor. Feeling too nervous to turn around and flee, I drove very slowly hoping they would just ignore me and let me pass, praying all the time that Benjamin would not wake up and start crying. Suddenly, one of the people from this group turned and started to run towards me. I could see in my headlights that it was a woman running with a baby in her arms. She was being chased by a man with a machete, and as she got close to me, the machete was swung down, hitting her straight on the back of the head. The baby was thrown from her arms and landed on the bonnet of my car. I was in complete shock, frozen to the spot. All I could think about was Benjamin in the back of the vehicle and what might happen if he woke up. I tentatively got out of the car to go and see if this baby who had rolled onto the ground was still alive. I picked the little bundle up and it started to whimper. Another man with a rifle came and joined us. He simply shot at the baby in my hands. I jumped so high and dropped the child. He then pointed the gun at my head but then seemed to have second thoughts, turned the rifle away and smashed my shoulder with the butt. He pushed me back into the car and yelled at me to go.

I have no idea how I managed to drive home but never have I been so thankful that Benjamin slept quietly through the entire ordeal. It was not until this happened that I recalled something a friend had shared with me many years earlier, long before I had any thoughts of going to Africa.

I was sitting in a church meeting in my home church in Cheam, and my friend Sheena shared a picture she felt God had given her. She saw me standing with a man who had a gun pointed at my head. She heard the Lord say, "I have snatched you from the brink of death and there will be times again when you will face death but you will not be afraid because you will know that I am with you." It seemed a rather unsettling picture with an odd word to go with it but I felt that it was a word from God, even though I had no idea what it meant. Now here I was, years later, in the middle of Africa, recalling that prophetic word as if it were yesterday. Why did I have to experience that? I have no idea, but God is God and one day I will understand it all.

It was a long time before I felt I could go out again after dark and I did not realize that within a very short time I would not be visiting the camps any more. Things were about to change.

CHAPTER 5

CRIB (CHILDREN RESCUED IN BURUNDI)

As I continued working in the camp, it quickly became clear to me that the babies and very young children were the most vulnerable of the displaced people. Any child who was too young, too traumatized, or too sick to stand in a line for food distribution just did not survive. Heartbreakingly, every day there seemed to be another baby or child to bury.

I recall how one day we were packing up to go home and I walked past a rubbish dump nearby. I spotted a baby who appeared to have been thrown there and abandoned. What else could I do? I scooped up the baby girl and took her home. That was the beginning. I didn't hear a great booming voice from heaven telling me to start an orphanage. I was just doing what my hands found to do. Within that one week in late 1994, I had managed to "collect" seventeen babies, all of them under six months old. I got some beanbags and the babies slept on them in rows in my sitting room.

I desperately tried to get some help at home with the babies. It was a case of the one that cried the loudest got fed first! Many were dehydrated and weak. I don't think I had more than two hours' sleep a night in the weeks that followed. I couldn't go to the camps any more because the camp had literally moved into my house!

Somehow, word spread that I had started a home for babies, and more duly appeared on my doorstep on a daily basis. I felt like a baby magnet. They were found in the most amazing places, often with no known relatives. Where a mother had been killed, many families had nobody to look after and feed the young children. It was an incredible situation and I felt completely overwhelmed.

One morning I felt exhausted. I had been up all night and I remember standing on my doorstep crying out to God and asking Him what to do. The need was so great but how could I possibly cope with any more babies? What was I going to do with these little bundles in my living room and how was I going to manage? God spoke to me very clearly but gently. I heard Him say, "Chrissie, if you can find room in your heart, you'll always find room in your house."

The full realization of why God had made a way for us to rent this big house was now very clear. It was like turning the clock back and starting all over again. It was one thing to be able to put babies on beanbags who are too young, too small, or too ill to move, but soon those beanbags were not going to work as beds. We were obviously going to have to look for a carpenter to make some cribs and to sort out the supply of such things as milk formula, baby clothes, and of course nappies (no such luxury as disposable nappies in Burundi!). Before too long everything started to come together. Friends back in the UK from my church in Cheam rose to the occasion and in no time at all, a container was shipped out full of prams, baby clothes, and nappies that they had collected and donated. They filled our empty shelves, which then enabled Rosa and I to concentrate on the babies rather than hunting for supplies. I also managed to get a good deal on baby milk formula from a company in the UK and arranged to have milk shipped out at regular intervals. With supplies arriving and Rosa heading up the team of our newly employed house mothers, we opened our doors to Burundi. CRIB was officially in business!

Most of the babies that had arrived that first week were not actually from the camp. I still have no real idea how people found out about this white missionary lady who was saving babies. One of the first babies to arrive was a small boy who we estimated to be about ten months old. He was found sitting on the doorstep of the Catholic church in the town centre by a night guard. He was taken to one of the camps and a lady with several children of her own took him in. However, after about two months, her husband told her she had to find someone else to take the child. It was just too difficult to have an extra mouth to feed when it was a daily struggle to feed your own. So the baby was brought to me. The lady in the camp had called the little boy Ngabire, which in Kirundi simply means "the gift". While he was in good health, we had no way at all of being able to trace any family members when a baby had been abandoned in such a way as Ngabire had. After he had been with us for about two months, a lady from the church came to visit. She had lost her husband and children and was keen to adopt a baby to try and fill the great void in her own life. She chose Ngabire. She came several times to play with him and let him get to know her, and eventually after a couple of weeks, we allowed her to take him home. We used to see him in church on Sunday mornings and everything seemed to be working out well. However, after a few months we lost contact with him until one day, our staff recognized Ngabire (who had by this time been given the new name, Moise which means Moses), running around the grounds of the hospital next to the church looking bedraggled and unkempt. His new mother had unfortunately developed tuberculosis and died. Once again, now aged almost two years old, he came back to us – and this time he stayed.

Another time, a little girl was found in a cardboard box buried under a pile of dried grass and leaves. It was thought that she had probably been hidden by her family as they fled from danger one night. The plan had probably been to go back and retrieve her when things were safe. But no one made it back to that village. This little girl was one of the saddest I had ever seen. She looked about eighteen months old, had a large pot belly and legs that were set straight so that she couldn't move them very much. She didn't smile and simply looked at us with a sad and fearful gaze. We called her Leah. It was quite obvious looking at this little girl that she was not only very traumatized but also quite unwell. After several trips to the hospital for all manner of tests, Leah was found to be HIV positive. She also had a very enlarged liver and no one really seemed to know why or what had caused it. We were not given much advice from the doctors at this point about what to do – and not much hope either. We therefore took her home, loved her and watched over her and prayed for her. She grew into a wonderful young lady. She was well into her teenage years when she began to fall prey to illness more often. She had problems with her liver condition and needed regular blood transfusions for anaemia. She loved life and had one big ambition: to reach eighteen years old – she just wanted to be an adult. She couldn't wait for her eighteenth birthday and that was a day of great celebration. She loved Jesus and wanted to do everything she could to please Him. One New Year's Eve she got baptized. However, her health continued to deteriorate and she was in and out of hospital. The time came, in April 2013, when she was too weak and anaemic to function at home and was finally admitted to hospital. Early one morning she sat up in bed and said to Rosa who was with her, "I think today I'm going to go and be with Jesus." Rosa was quite shocked and not knowing quite what to say, asked her, "Do you want to phone anybody to tell them?" Leah said yes, she wanted to phone everybody and tell them that she was going. Then, she simply laid back down on the pillow and left us; she just decided that this was the day she was going to meet Jesus face to face – just five months before her twentieth birthday.

In the early days, we lost a number of young babies either to AIDS-related illnesses or else to malnourishment or even just the pitiful state the babies arrived in. However, the majority survived. The babies that arrived in those early days each have their own stories to tell.

One baby was found at just a few weeks old, wrapped in a blanket under a bush in the car park of a restaurant. Another one was found in a shopping basket at the side of the road. We had babies who were simply abandoned; parents assumed killed. Many hid their babies under trees or in places they thought would be safe. Time and time again, however, no one returned and these babies would be found by passers-by who heard them crying.

I had a phone call one day from the hospital about a young boy who had accompanied his mother and baby brother to the hospital. Unfortunately, his mother and brother had both died. Murungwa (later John) was just eight years old. The family had been in one of the camps where cholera and typhoid had claimed many victims. The young boy had been left at the hospital for several days after his mother had died and when asked, didn't know if he had any other relatives. He was therefore just left there. We went to the hospital and brought him home. When he had been with us for about two years, his grandmother and two other brothers and a sister arrived to take him. John, however, decided he wanted to stay at CRIB as he was settled and enjoying school. He has kept in touch with his family over the years and visits them at regular intervals.

Another time a missionary friend appeared on our doorstep with a young girl who was carrying her baby brother, John Paul. Their mother had died in childbirth leaving this thirteen-year-old girl to look after the baby. The girl, Fabiola, said she thought her father had died a few months earlier because he just disappeared one day. The baby boy was six weeks old and weighed just 3 kg. She had kept him alive by giving him black tea, birds' eggs, and squeezing the juice from bananas. This little boy was one of the most malnourished babies I had ever seen and I doubted that he would survive. Fabiola had walked about 20 km from up in the mountains to get to the city to try and save her brother's life. She also looked quite unwell herself. We had her checked out at the hospital and she was found to have malaria, amoebic dysentery, and typhoid. What could I do other than open my door and invite them in?

In the end I had to come up with some kind of criteria for whom I could accept into CRIB because the needs were so vast and I knew I couldn't take each and every one that came knocking at my door. I felt very strongly that I needed to concentrate on babies with no living female relative to look after them: mostly babies under a year old and still needing milk. Also, I felt I had to take in vulnerable children under five years old who were either sick or badly traumatized. These children weren't able to survive in the camps. Of course, there were times when we had to make an exception to the rule and Fabiola was one of these exceptions. Fabiola loves Jesus, as does John Paul, who survived against all odds and is grateful to Jesus and his big sister for saving his life. After a few years of being with us, they did discover their father and two sisters were still alive but decided to stay on with us at CRIB.

Almost on a daily basis, we had folk at our gate clutching babies and small children, asking if we would take the children and give them a chance of survival. It was heart-rending to hear some of the stories the women would tell. They were desperate to find a way to keep their children alive and distraught at the sound of them crying continually because of hunger. On occasion, some of these children would be found eating dirt to try and stop the pain of hunger pangs so they could sleep. Although I couldn't take babies or children who had a mother to care for them, I couldn't turn them away without offering them anything either. We therefore started yet another project to feed people who turned up at CRIB. We never did turn anyone away without first feeding them. Day after day people came and we would give them *ubuyi*, beans, or rice and some dried food to take away to cook when they had got back to the camp. These mothers could at least leave without hearing their precious little ones groaning with hunger, for a few nights at least.

Donations kept coming in, either by way of money so that we could buy more food, or in the form of food. One of the aid organizations we applied to locally donated sacks of maize flour and dried peas and somehow, no matter how many people came to the door, we always seemed to have enough. We were living in a miracle. I am amazed at how many hundreds of mothers and children we were able to save and help. I never had to worry about whether we would have enough as there always was enough. As we continued to channel what God had given us, He continued to replenish our storehouse again and again. In fact, for over twenty years, right to this day, we have always had just as much as we need (and sometimes more) and our policy is still the same: we never turn anyone away hungry.

Most of the babies who came to us were either sent from the hospitals that had come to know us quite well, or via missionary friends who had a clinic and a small camp of displaced people who had settled on their mission land. We were the only place in Burundi at that time which was helping babies. The government orphanage was full to overflowing. In fact, for two years we took a truck of fresh fruit and vegetables to the government orphanage every week out of the overflow of what we had. We just kept giving.

Once there was a call from our mission hospital asking if we could take a baby boy of about eleven months old. His mother was ill and unable to cope with him. He was in fact almost dead, suffering with malnutrition, when he arrived at the hospital. After about a week of treatment, the mother who was a single girl, left in the middle of the night, leaving her baby behind. He was doing much better but he had scoliosis and a very curved spine. He found it difficult to sit up without falling over and just lay curled on his side. However, Francois was bright-eyed and seemed to be feeding quite well and recovering from the acute malnutrition and dehydration. Once again, here was another little boy who came to join our CRIB family and remains with us still.

Another day, another hospital, another phone call... could we take a five-day-old baby girl? This was the nurse in charge of the intensive care baby unit at one of the large public hospitals in the city. This baby had been found by a nurse down a toilet in the hospital; she was just a few hours old. She weighed a mere 2 kg and was thought to be about three to four weeks premature. This vulnerable little baby still had the umbilical cord attached and although very cold, was amazingly still alive. She looked perfect. They kept her in an incubator for five days to warm her up and gave her some strong antibiotics to guard against infection because of being found in such an unsterile location. She took milk quite well from a spoon: there being no such things as feeding bottles in African hospitals.

We went to the hospital to collect this exquisite little bundle and we called her Grace. It seemed her survival had been due to the grace of God so she had to have that name!

Not long after this, another young girl arrived at the camp where my friend worked, along with her two baby brothers. This girl, who was thought to be about eleven years old, told us that her mother had died after giving birth to her baby brother. Just a few hours old, she brought Able along with another brother, Ciza, who looked about twenty months old. The baby looked reasonably well but the twenty-month-old was obviously suffering quite badly from protein-deficiency malnutrition. He had very swollen limbs and a kind of rusty-coloured hair, which is a typical symptom of lack of protein. He also had a high fever and was crying uncontrollably. Seeing white people, probably for the first time in his life, didn't help to calm this poor child. We did not get much of a history of any other family members; the father was said to have died several months previously and the whereabouts of any other family was unknown. We took in the two babies and my friend took the young girl with her to see if maybe they could try and trace any other family. Often we discovered that if there had been an attack in a particular area, people fled in every direction and tended to stay hidden for several days or weeks at a time until they felt safe again. They would then make their way back to their homes and often get reunited with other family members and neighbours that had been assumed killed.

Both of these baby boys cried all night and made more noise than all the other babies put together! We needed to get the twenty-month-old to the hospital. It was discovered that he had malaria very badly. We sent for his older sister to come and stay in the hospital with him as he needed to have intravenous fluids and medicines to treat the malaria. He was in hospital for about a week and during that time no other relatives were tracked down. So, once again, another exception to the unwritten rule: we took these three children home with us. Nizigiyimana, Ciza, and Able together came to be part of the CRIB family.

It was quite a number of years later that the children's grandmother turned up on our doorstep, as well as another brother who had survived. It never ceases to amaze me that over and over again sometimes years will elapse after we have taken a baby in, and then, out of the blue, long-lost relatives turn up at CRIB. This is not a rare occurrence for children in our care. Some have even reached teenage years and an aunt, uncle, or even a father appears, somehow having found out that the baby they thought was dead, is in fact still alive and a boisterous teenager! Of course, it was wonderful for the children in our care to be able to find some information about who they were and who their family was. It helps to bring some identity and somehow closure to a lot of unanswered questions, but so far none of the children have wanted to leave CRIB and go back to live with relatives. To visit them in the school holidays is fine but CRIB is family for them: here are the brothers and sisters they have grown up with, laughed and cried with, and at times fought with! CRIB is home for quite a while longer while they discover and pursue their dreams and work out exactly what they want to do with the life God has rescued them for.

Another small boy who joined us for just a brief time was Eliah. Such a sad and pathetic sight was this little boy. We estimated that from his teeth and also from his vocabulary that he must have been at least four years old but he was so malnourished that he fitted into the pyjamas of an eighteen-month-old. He had obviously been neglected for months and was found abandoned under a tree. He could have been just wandering around alone for months. He was covered in sores and was barely alive; so fragile, it was hard to even touch him without causing pain and distress. For four days he could hardly tolerate anything but small amounts of sugar water and a little bit of warm milk. All he wanted was to hold a small bag of peanuts in his hand. He couldn't eat them and hardly had the strength to hold them but he seemed to take comfort in holding this bag of peanuts.

One morning he was sitting in a highchair and one of the workers was trying to get him to eat a few spoons of porridge, but as I looked at him it was as if the light had gone out in eyes. I just knew that this was one life I was not going to be able to save. As I looked, I felt God say to me, "Give him a party." Although we mostly had babies who were not old enough to be aware of what was going on around them, we also had several children who would realize if Eliah wasn't there any more. So, with tears rolling down my face, I made a cake and some cookies and after the lunchtime nap, we took Eliah into the garden and laid him on a mattress under the mango tree. The other children came out as well and we taught them about Jesus and about heaven. We told Eliah it was OK and he could go and be with Jesus in heaven and feel better. We had a goodbye party. The adults all cried and the children all laughed; they were so excited and asked if there would be jelly in heaven. Children are so trusting. It never occurred to them that this small boy would not be with us after today. He was going on a wonderful journey to heaven to finish his party with Jesus where he could eat as much jelly as he wanted.

Over a few weeks we had a whole run of very young and very sick babies arriving. One of the bedrooms looked like a hospital at one point as I had to attach intravenous drips to a number of babies who were too weak, too sick, and too dehydrated to drink. We had Cedric who was about five months old; Gwego, six weeks old; Joseph, six days old; Eveline, five weeks old; Peter, three weeks old; Maria, two weeks old; Ruth, ten days old; Josiah, a week old. Over a period of a couple of weeks, all these babies passed out of my arms and into the arms of Jesus. There were times when I felt so completely helpless and overwhelmed. Many of these little ones were HIV positive. Sometimes when we felt like closing our doors because it was just so hard to think about losing another baby, another baby would arrive but would be encouragingly healthy and hungry.

We had two such arrive on the same day: Samuel and David, both just over a week old and both in good health. Samuel's mother had died after giving birth; David was found abandoned. It was quite a blessing for us to have a couple of chubby babies to cuddle after all the losses we had experienced.

Another day we had a very unusual little boy arrive. He was about six or seven years old, was dressed, and looked like a little old man. He was like most of the children who came to us: malnourished and desperately neglected; he had no idea where he was from or what had happened to his family. With no history, this was yet another child with no traceable family. When I think of all the children who came to CRIB, Budusy was probably one of the most traumatized. He settled in well enough but over the years never seemed to connect well with any of the other children. He seemed to like school and was reasonably bright but was quiet and withdrawn. It took many years for this young man to eventually experience real friendships. As he has continued over the years to choose Jesus, he is all the time walking into new levels of freedom and friendships.

As many babies and children continued to arrive on our doorstep, we did actually have to send more away than we took in. It was such a difficult and challenging task to decide who should come to stay and to whom we should say no. Over a period of time, we started to get a little suspicious of some of the ladies who would turn up and try to hand over babies to us. They would say that the baby's mother had died or they had found the baby abandoned, when in fact on some occasions it was more than a little obvious that the child was their own! I couldn't blame them for trying. At first I just couldn't understand how any mother could possibly want to give her baby away but eventually I realized that this was a sacrifice in order to try and ensure the child would survive. The depth of love these mothers had for their infants and the desperation they experienced trying to find milk or food to keep them from starving was moving indeed.

War is a terrible thing to live through and what these widows and orphans suffered was also a war: the ongoing torment of hunger and disease without any respite. To give these dear ladies some bread, tea, and some milk for their little ones, you could truly not have blessed them any more if you had given them vast riches. There is a verse in Psalm 16 that says "The boundary lines have fallen to me in pleasant places" (verse 6, NIV). What a wonderful inheritance we have. What an amazing blessing it is to be born in a First World country. I will never have to suffer like many people born in the Third World have to. I will never suffer poverty like the poverty and hardship seen here. No matter how hard it gets, I know for sure that we are blessed because the boundary lines have fallen for us in pleasant places. To be content is to have a thankful heart and to acknowledge the blessings God gives. It is so easy when going through trials to take our eyes off God and His wonderful provision, such as a place to sleep, adequate food, and access to medical care if we need it. It never occurred to me before I came to Africa that every day thousands of people do not enjoy any of these things. Still, so many manage to find Jesus in the midst of such poverty and to know the reality of what it really means to say grace and give thanks before eating. They are more truly thankful than we could ever imagine.

At times, it feels like the scales are so unfairly balanced but I have come to see that the lack of even the most basic material possessions seems to leave a clear and uncluttered path to Jesus and His eternal riches. They love Him, not for what He can give them, but simply for who He is.

So many children and so many stories… There was a day when I received a call to ask if I could send our vehicle to the Rwandan border to help bring some survivors of the Rwandan genocide to the city. I contacted a friend who was willing to go and see what help he could offer. On arrival at the border, we found there were hundreds of people trying to get lifts into the city in order to get to one of the refugee camps. My friend John concentrated his attentions on collecting up the most vulnerable and weak, which were mainly the children and babies. He also found a lady lying by the road with a new baby. She had gone into labour while she was running and had given birth to a healthy baby boy at the side of the road. She joined the children in our vehicle and somehow ended up on a mattress in my office, surrounded by terrified, traumatized, and hungry children.

Over the months that followed, being with the children was like watching blocks of ice slowly melting. To begin with, they would just sit quite still, seemingly frozen with no smile or eye contact. We found that a routine was very important and tried to create a peaceful environment where they could feel safe, which was not always easy with the sounds of bomb blasts and shooting outside and at times distressed screaming infants inside! But each morning I would put on a quiet worship tape and soft music seemed to bring calmness to the house.

Many of these little ones would not allow us to cuddle them. They couldn't cope with being touched or picked up too often but slowly as the days passed and we gave them time to come to a place of trust, we began to see some changes. For some, it was a little smile when milk or food appeared. Others would allow one of the other children to hold them. Some of the children, even as young as three years old, seemed to sense what these toddlers were experiencing and they would gently go and sit beside these emotionally frozen babies and sit and stroke them and then pick them up. It was not unusual to find a small child sitting quietly in a corner, cuddling a baby. One time, as I looked in the face of a fifteen-month-old baby being cuddled by a four-year-old, I saw her eyes were closed but huge, silent tears flowed down her tiny traumatized face. I knew that God was using that four-year-old to be a vessel of healing. What God had done in these older children He was now doing through them. It was an indescribable feeling when, one by one, these little children began to recover.

One day, a little boy of about a year old, tentatively raised his hands towards me indicating that I could pick him up. As I looked at him, it was as if he was saying, you can pick me up but be very careful, I'm very fragile. As I held him in my arms, I could feel a deep sigh and then deep, deep sobs that came from somewhere deep inside his small body. Eventually he became still and quiet again and he found his smile and he was changed. The thriving process had started.

As I say, what we witnessed in these children was that as they got through the trauma of their experiences, they seemed to automatically be drawn to any new babies and children who came into CRIB. They would sit with them and what had taken weeks or months in the past to get little ones settled and through the terrible screams and terrors that seemed to come with the darkness of night, now was only taking days until they could feel peace. The whole process of inner healing seemed to have been speeded up as the children ministered by simply reaching out and loving each other, without the use of words.

As the house got fuller, it seemed to get smaller: every room was packed wall-to-wall with cribs and rows of prams, and beanbags all over the sitting room containing sleeping babies. This large house now seemed to have shrunk. Once again I started to pray and ask God for direction to know what to do next, and once again He revealed His plan and made a way for us to buy this big house.

The director of an organization who had been helping us with some finance to buy food came to visit and, after long discussions, his organization released the finance needed to buy this property, which meant that we could now look at how to expand. It also meant that we no longer had to pay the rent that God had continued to graciously provide over the last few years. So with the house now belonging to the charity, the next step was to get a plan of action for some kind of extension. I came up with the idea of building a baby unit in the garden. One of God's promises to us is that He will provide for all of our needs – and He certainly did. He sent not one but two young ladies from the UK to help out with the everyday care of the children. There was Libby, a highly educated English girl whom I had met when she was taking a gap year after her A levels. She wanted to study medicine but God had directed her to Burundi to help us. The other girl was Annelie, a newly qualified registered nurse from Scotland, who also joined us and we were very grateful they both did.

Through a whole series of events, including my speaking at churches in Canada, I met Pastors Ray and Mary Anne Bale, which culminated in a whole team coming out to Burundi from different parts of Canada. Ray brought with him men connected to the Salt & Light churches who had building skills. The Lord provided the finances and a building team and our brand new four-bedroom baby unit was built in the record time of six weeks.

As the unit was now filled with cribs and the babies moved in, for the first time in a little over two years, I got a full night's sleep. It was quite strange to wake up to the sight of daylight, but desperately needed and a wonderful feeling!

Of course, as the time passed, we ran out of space again, so, in January 1998, the next step was to rent an additional house, which we simply called House 2. Libby and Annelie moved into this house and took the first group of toddlers with them. It was just a five minute walk from the main house, which we called House 1. A pattern was now followed. As soon as the babies no longer needed bottle feeding and had started to eat solids (usually between the ages of fifteen to eighteen months' old), we moved them from the baby unit to make more room for more babies and into House 2. In the end, we had Houses 1 and 2, then House 3, and then House 4! When we got to House 5, it was time to start thinking and planning and seeking God for what was the next step. Renting additional houses and paying staff and the bills to cover all of the houses was not going to be feasible for much longer. Time to pray and seek God again for the next step in my journey.

CHAPTER 6

MIRACLE AFTER MIRACLE

As the weeks passed and the babies thrived, life remained very busy with many comings and goings. The turnover of the house mothers we employed was quite extensive because of the demands of the work. Keeping up with the laundry and washing nappies by hand for so many children was a full-time job for one person. Most of the babies also had medical and emotional needs, which presented us with even more challenges. Baby Grace, the girl who had been found abandoned down a toilet and came to us when she was five days old, survived against all the odds. She was not an easy baby: she didn't feed well at all. It would often take over an hour to get a couple of ounces of milk into her. She didn't seem to know how to suck properly and we mostly had to feed her milk with a teaspoon, which took such a long time. She often seemed to have a faraway look on her face and was not particularly responsive to us. She was slow to smile and for a baby, was far too quiet.

After a few months, I took her to see a doctor to try and discover what was ailing this little baby. The doctor performed a thorough medical check on her, which included all kinds of blood tests and also a hearing test. To my dismay, it was discovered that she was profoundly deaf in both ears. The conclusion given was that this had probably been caused by large doses of an antibiotic called Gentamicin. This had been administered to Grace when she was first born, due to the insanitary conditions of where she had been found and was a preventative measure against infection. Sadly, one of the possible side-effects of this antibiotic is deafness if the levels administered are too high. Little Grace was healthy enough and infection free, but seemingly profoundly deaf.

One afternoon, the pastor from my church came to visit. Pastor Edmund was a friend and often came to visit to pray for the children. I sat and told him Grace's story (she was about eight months at this time) and afterwards he asked if he could pray for her. He felt moved to anoint her with oil; however, all I had was some cooking oil, so that had to do! He prayed earnestly for her and anointed her with a small drop of oil in each ear. A few days passed and we could not understand why Grace who had been so quiet and withdrawn, was now very restless and agitated and was crying almost continuously. It was so unusual for her and she seemed particularly disturbed during the daytime. One afternoon her screaming and crying became too much so I took her to my bedroom away from all the other children to try and get her to settle and maybe sleep. She eventually lay quietly and after a short while, my little son Benjamin came crawling into the room, banging the door behind him. Poor Grace almost jumped a foot in the air with shock. It was then that I realized what the problem was: she could hear! My goodness, after months of being in her own little world of soundless solitude, all of a sudden, I realized that God had healed her. The noise of all the other babies crying and worship music playing had terrified this little girl who had never heard these sounds before. For about a week, we put small cotton wool pads in her ears to help her as she got accustomed to our noisy household. Later, as a toddler, Grace and some of the other children in our care whom God had healed would lovingly embrace the new babies and children who came into the home. Time and time again, we saw that what God had done in them, he was now doing through them. Their contact and presence with the other children seemed to bring a wonderful sense of peace and healing.

Murungwa, who came to us from the hospital where his mother and baby brother had died, was one of the hardest working boys I have known. Almost from the minute he arrived, he was determined to study as hard as he could and had a dream that one day he would make it to university. Even after members of his family turned up when he had been with us for a few months, he set his mind to stay with us at CRIB and to study. He wanted to stay in school and all his hard work eventually paid off.

Fabiola, the teenage girl who came to us sick and exhausted with her baby brother, John Paul, in tow, had only one plan, which was to survive and to try and save her brother's life. It took weeks to get John Paul into a stable place where he could actually drink milk in any reasonable amount. He slowly started to gain weight. Fabiola recovered well after getting the correct medical treatment for her health issues. She was another young person who was determined to work hard and put all her energy into studying with such an earnest desire to succeed and make something of her life. These young people who had come to us, having survived the war and often seeing family members die, seemed to enthusiastically embrace the fact that they had been given a second chance in life.

I feel the stories of these children need to be told. You may ask what is so miraculous about young people reaching their dreams after working hard and obtaining a university degree? It happens all the time to so many young people. The miracle for these whose stories I tell, is that they survived when hundreds around them perished in the genocide; against all the odds they made it and made it with a sound mind. They chose to take hold of their past and turn it into a future. To be a witness to the grace of God at work in the lives of these children has been the most awesome privilege for me. To see God's favour in the midst of death and destruction is indeed a miracle.

We have had our share of some of the most amazing healing miracles. You may remember Francois who came to us as a baby. He had such severe scoliosis that he couldn't sit up as his back was so bent and his spine so curved. Of course, here in Africa, we had no way of being able to offer any hope of corrective surgery to rectify the problem. We were told to lie Francois on his stomach and to tie his hands and feet to the ends of his bed for a couple of hours each day to see if that would help to straighten his little bent back. Of course, we respectfully disregarded those instructions: far too distressing and painful for a baby to endure. Francois either sat bent forward or lay on his side, curled up – that was his life. Then came the afternoon when childlike faith came to life. Little Grace, about four at this time, and some of her little band of followers, decided that they would pray for Francois. It was like watching a game of pat-a-cake, pat-a-cake as they patted him, pushed him, and sent up all sorts of mumbles and childlike prayers. After a while Francois became quite distressed from all the well-intentioned patting and was put down for his afternoon nap. After a couple of hours he was brought outside into the sunshine again. It seemed that there was something different about him that no one could quite work out. Then someone noticed that he was standing up and had a rare smile on his face. On closer inspection, his back was no longer bent – it was quite straight. His spine was no longer curved. He was healed and Jesus was the only one who could possibly have done that. To the children, it was no big deal. What was all the fuss about, it was just another day!

My desire was that all who came to us with such problems could be healed just like this, but often it did not always happen in this way. The healing power of Jesus is something that people have been discussing and debating for centuries. There are probably more questions than there are answers. I myself have experienced God's touch and have been healed in a miraculous way on more than one occasion. If God had not healed me from chronic lung problems and asthma, I never could have come to Africa. I have also known what it is like not to be healed and have had more than my fair share of major surgery over the years. I have seen with my own eyes people healed as I have prayed for them, but I have had many children and babies die in my arms even after praying for healing. I steadfastly believe, however, that whatever the outcome, prayer is never a waste of time. I will never not pray and reach out to God for healing. Whatever the end result, that is up to God, but there is nothing anyone can do that will convince me that God does not heal. It is too late, I have seen too much. My own lovely daughter, Hannah, healed from being HIV positive, which as we know, carries a death sentence, to HIV negative and a prognosis of a healthy long life. God's touch on her occurred as she lay in my arms at eight months. No great long healing prayers, just an exhausted, desperate mama who loved her baby, loved Jesus, and believed all things were possible – so simple yet so profound.

As I mentioned earlier, here in Africa, it is a regular occurrence that miracles happen. Deaf ears are opened, blind eyes see, and often the lame walk. There are adults who have been healed from AIDS – not many, but it happens. They can show you their test paper from the laboratory that states "HIV positive" and then the new report, "HIV negative". They are a minority but that does not mean that we do not pray for everyone who comes in search of healing, because they may well experience the next miracle of that day.

We see and learn as we observe Jesus at work and that He is who He says He is: the one with healing in His wings. He is the same yesterday, today, and forever. We see that faith rises and it is contagious as the Holy Spirit begins to move and healings start to happen. It is often like a huge wave: it starts slowly and builds up until it reaches its peak and crashes down on the beach. Often a whole group or section of people will experience the touch of God: feel a presence and have a sense that something profound is about to happen. Blind eyes see and deaf ears are open, fevers break, and captives are released, and all manner of ailments disappear. People are left with no doubt that Jesus has just passed that way.

The Scriptures come alive at times such as this. Take for instance the woman with the issue of blood in Matthew 9:20–22. For twelve years this woman had been ill and had probably spent everything she had to try and find a cure for her problem. The healing she needed was not just physical – she also experienced terrible stigma and shame for her condition, which had kept her confined for those twelve long years. Somehow, she heard about Jesus and that He could heal people. I can imagine that, at the end of her tether, she took a bold step of faith and followed the crowd who were heading to see this man, Jesus. She told herself, "I don't even need Him to touch me, if I could just touch the fringe of His cloak, everything will be OK." She did and it *was* OK. She pushed through her own disgrace and embarrassment and got down low, squeezing through the crowd to reach out and touch the fringe of Jesus' cloak. Jesus felt at that moment that life had gone out of Him. He turned and simply told her, "Your faith has healed you." In other words, it was you who took your healing which I freely give to all who come. It is the same Jesus who has the same power to heal today. If only we could reach out just far enough to touch His hem.

What we experienced in our CRIB home with all the babies, traumatized children, and the many sick who came to our door, was that as the worship music flowed and quiet prayer was offered up, little by little things changed. The deep emotional traumas some of these children had experienced caused them to have night screams or to experience great panic at any sudden noise or movement. Some just seemed to freeze, sitting with vacant faces, staring into space, not responding or reacting to anything or anyone. Over a period of time, sometimes weeks or months, slowly change started to occur as fear and terror began to seep away. We noticed as the months passed that some of the new babies and children who came in had the same emotional problems as some of the ones who had been healed of all their traumas. As these new ones came and were added to our family, they seemed to come into an atmosphere of love and peace, calm and wholeness and wellbeing, and we saw that what used to take weeks and sometimes months to get these children to a place of calm, now only seemed to take days or sometimes weeks. It was as if the whole process had been speeded up; it was as if we were building walls of peace and healing and the children naturally entered into that. There are really no words to describe or explain adequately what was happening but we knew that Jesus was at work in our midst and miracles were indeed occurring as when He walked this earth.

All of these experiences over what is now almost twenty-five years in Africa have taught me that if any one of us turns and seeks Him with all of our hearts, He is there to be found. He really is the same yesterday, today, and forever (Hebrews 13:8).

CHAPTER 7

A BAD WEEK

In all the years I have lived in Burundi I have certainly had my share of narrow escapes. However, there is one week that stands out in my memory as being the mother of all weeks! I'm sure we have all had bad days, but this for me really was a week to remember.

In September 1995 my youngest daughter Hannah was almost three years old. The big day arrived when she was to start nursery school. She was so excited and very much looking forward to going. Lydia, her big sister, was also attending the same school but was in the primary section. School started at 7.30 a.m. and ended at 12.00 noon for nursery and infants, and at 1.00 p.m. for primary children. My morning at home seemed to go relatively slowly as I eagerly awaited midday when Hannah would return with what I hoped would be a positive account of how she had got on. I started to prepare a special lunch for when she returned.

I thought about how small she had looked that morning as she left with her little backpack, a new drinking bottle, a snack, and her favourite handkerchief embroidered with a small flower in the corner. She had felt so grown up as she had left hand-in-hand with Lydia. Benjamin and I waved them off as Alexi our house boy walked the ten-minute journey with them to school.

Alexi duly went to collect Hannah but my heart sank when he arrived home a little later, not with an excited Hannah in tow, but alone. He told me Hannah was nowhere to be seen. With a sense of panic, I handed Benjamin over to one of the house mothers and jumped into my car to race the short distance to the school. Over the next few hours it seemed like a nightmare was unfolding as I talked to the school's director to try and ascertain where Hannah was. The class teacher had handed Hannah over to a man who told her that Hannah's mother had been delayed at work and had asked him to collect her. The teacher thought nothing of it and allowed Hannah to go with him. However, when she got as far as the man's car, it seemed that she became upset because the school guard reported that he had noticed a small girl crying and talking in English. He was able to describe the colour of the car and the sticker it had on the back window. He was also able to guess at the make and model of the car and (amazingly, considering the amount of traffic) noticed the direction in which the car was going. By this time, it was 1 p.m. and Lydia had now finished school. It was decided that I would take Lydia home and at the same time bring Rosa, our house mother, who I thought could help me with any Kirundi interpretation needed, back with me. We returned to the school to collect the school director and a police officer. We then took off in the direction the car had been headed: towards a housing estate not far from the school.

The area we were searching consisted of rows of houses all backing onto each other and connected with narrow dirt roads. We drove slowly, looking over all the gates and trying to peer into every compound, searching for a dark blue saloon car with a small sticker in the corner of the back window. After two hours hope was beginning to fade. All of a sudden we spotted it – a dark blue saloon with a sticker. I almost broke the gate down and ran towards the open door of the house where I could see Hannah. Ironically, she looked happy and was covered in green *sombe* (a kind of spinach dish eaten with rice which is very common in Burundi). She had a colouring book and pencils and did not seem at all troubled. My pent-up emotions seemed to explode and it took quite a long time to calm me down. The policeman and school director managed to restrain me from manhandling this man who stood and stared at me as if I were a mad woman! He dubiously explained that his friends had asked him to collect their child and he had mistakenly thought that the child was Hannah. But where was the other child and where were their supposed parents?

A decision was made that I would take Hannah home and the man who had taken her would go and get the mother of the child he was supposed to have collected (big mistake). This was a case of mistaken identity I was told. We would then all meet back at the school with senior police officers and try and unravel this crazy scenario. I was just so relieved to have Hannah back, happy and healthy. However, I felt emotionally exhausted and I was willing to do whatever I was advised by the officials. So, home we went, calmed down, had a drink, and went back off to school, leaving the children safely at home while we tried to make sense of what had happened and to make sure that this situation could never happen again. We all waited at school for a while and doubts started to come to the surface concerning the wisdom of letting this man go. Eventually, the police went back to the house to find that the man had gone, together with the car, and almost all the personal contents of the house. This had obviously been a scam. There was no mistaken identity. It was thought that Hannah possibly had been kidnapped because I was white, and therefore assumed wealthy and in a position to pay a large amount of reward money in return for my daughter. This whole situation left me shell-shocked. My head was filled with all the "what ifs". What if the school guard hadn't noticed the blue car? What if we hadn't found Hannah? What if the same people came back? On and on these thoughts went around my head. I thank God that Hannah had no idea at all about what had happened. She had loved school and had enjoyed her *sombe* lunch and thought that it was all part of a normal day at school. In fact, as I tucked her up in bed later on that Monday evening, she asked me, "Am I going to the nice house again tomorrow for some *sombe*?"!

There was no way of tracing the people who were responsible for abducting Hannah or to ascertain why she was targeted. The country was at the height of civil war with so much death and carnage all around that there was not much interest or indeed time for the police to investigate this situation in any depth. These things happen and mistakes can be made, I was told. I was determined that it was not going to happen to my children ever again. It was quite difficult to know what to do. I wondered if I should keep the children at home as I wasn't sure that they would be safe to go back to school. After a sleepless night, I decided that I couldn't keep them in the house or away from school for ever. After much thought and prayer and a determination to carry on as normally as possible, I took the children to school the next morning and the teacher was given strict instructions that only myself or our guard and house boy, Alexi, could collect them.

At midday the next day (Tuesday), Hannah was back at school, happy and waiting for me to collect her. I expect she wondered what all the fuss had been about. We never experienced any such problem again. Life for me was never quite the same, though. I was always watching the clock and was unable to completely relax until school was over and all the children were home again safe and sound.

Wednesday of that week saw a lot of heavy gunfire and fighting in the city – not the kind of day to tempt you out of the house, except for essential errands. There was always a feeling of latent tension in the air, and quite understandably the house staff were very anxious and on edge. The sound of gunfire outside sometimes became too close for comfort. It was during the early hours of that morning that the gunfire became so loud and immediate that we all moved into the hallway of the house in case any stray bullet found its way through one of the bedroom windows. It was a terrifying experience but we attempted to keep calm so the children did not detect our panic. As we crouched in the darkness, suddenly the most almighty explosion shook the house. We sat frozen to the spot for what felt like hours, not daring to move. Fearful thoughts filled my mind: would there be gunmen in the garden outside? Was the house still in one piece? It was not until a few hours later when things became quiet again that we discovered the explosion had been the result of a grenade thrown into our grounds. It had thankfully missed the house but had hit and destroyed most of our back garden wall. God had protected us once again. On closer inspection, later that day, I saw dents in the window frame of my bedroom where a bullet had hit the frame but had missed the window. In fact, it was not actually we who were the targets of this attack, but we just happened to be in the middle of two warring groups.

As the sun rose once again, there were choices to be made. Do we stay inside and surrender to the fear that was trying to grip our hearts, or do we start the day once again praising God for His protection and carry on as normal? The latter was the only choice to be made for all of our sakes. The children would go to school as normal. I would find a builder to repair the wall. I would turn the worship tapes on and sing praises to God and get on with life. We were all alive and well. I chose to praise God, despite it all.

The next morning passed without incident. Lydia and Hannah attended school. I felt it was important, with all the uncertainty and instability in the country that we were calm and kept to some kind of routine as much as possible.

At school the children were distracted with activities and enjoyed being with their friends. At midday, Hannah was collected by Alexi and arrived home happy and ready for lunch. She then went for a nap. I sat on the front balcony helping Benjamin, who was about eighteen months old at the time, eat his lunch as he sat in his highchair. We were waiting for Lydia to return home and the rest of us looking forward to a well-deserved afternoon nap following lunch. The garden was full of babies in prams sleeping. Suddenly there was banging on the front gate.

At that time our front gate was not really very strong: it was a simple bamboo frame construction. The only wall we had was at the back of the house and there wasn't much of that left now following the grenade attack. The front and sides of our garden were bordered with hedges, about four-foot high. It was easy to see over the top and I saw a white minibus outside the gate. The man banging on the gate was holding a small parcel in his hand. As our guard had gone to collect Lydia, one of the house girls went to the gate to talk to him. The man knew my name and said he was delivering a gift to me. The house girl was hesitant to open the gate and asked him to pass the gift over the top of the gate. At that moment, the minibus crashed through the front gate and out jumped six armed gunmen! Two of them walked slowly toward me on the balcony. I nervously stood in front of Ben, trying to hide him. The other men ran around and within minutes had rounded up all the house girls, locked them in the bathroom within the house and then proceeded to throw the key in the garden. They had imprisoned all of them except for one girl who had been sitting under a tree in the garden feeding one of the babies.

When she realized something was happening, she started to run with the baby in her arms, jumped up over the hedge and into the next-door garden. While this was going on, the two men who were with me marched me into my bedroom. They seemed to know that I kept money in a drawer in my room but whoever they got their information from had misinformed them as they were convinced that I had a stash of US dollars in the house. It was bad news for me, and it was bad news for them, because they thought I was telling lies, when in actual fact there really was no money. The fact was I never had any dollars at all. They forced me face down onto the bedroom floor in what they call the execution position. This was the moment I thought I was going to take a short cut and go and be with Jesus. How could I survive this?

Well, at that moment a gunshot sounded from outside and the only thought in my head was that they had shot Benjamin. I jumped up without thinking and just ran, knocking both my attackers aside. I am not at all sure who was more shocked – me or them! They were equally nervous about the gunshot and ran after me to see what on earth was happening. As I ran out through the sitting room and onto the front balcony, I found Benjamin still in his highchair quite happily playing with a gun. One of these crazy bandits had given him a loaded gun to play with to keep him quiet. He had the end of it in his mouth – a novel teething ring to say the least! As we stood there in shock, they realized the gunshot had not come from any of them and already the bus was reversing back outside the gate to get away. All the men quickly jumped in and they were gone. The whole incident probably only lasted fifteen minutes, but to me it felt like a lifetime.

In fact, the gunshot had come from our neighbour's house. When the house girl had leapt into their garden and alerted them to what was happening, our neighbour, who kept a gun in his home, shot it into the air in an attempt to startle the bandits. Thankfully it worked. I managed to find the key and released the house girls from the bathroom. Soon after, Lydia arrived home wondering what on earth was happening and asked who had broken the gate down. Hannah had slept through it all.

We now needed both a new wall and a new gate. In fact we decided that a new wall would be built, not just at the back but also for security at the front as well. An eight-foot high wall and a huge strong gate were duly erected and I felt as if I were in prison. In the end nothing except a camera and a few videos were taken, snatched at the last minute as the gunmen ran to escape. However, this incident took its toll on me. My heart was now completely gripped with fear. I felt so confused and vulnerable. I didn't want to go out, but the events of the last few days made me fearful of staying in as well. I had to stay calm and hold myself together for the sake of everyone else. If I fell apart, I imagined everyone else would follow suit and I couldn't risk that. I had a house full of babies, terrified housemothers, workers, and me. I felt as if I was in the middle of a horrific nightmare that I couldn't wake up from. That night, I got little sleep and felt on edge, almost waiting for the next incident to occur.

Thursday was just a blur. We somehow managed to get through the day. I was scared to let the children go to school now but also scared to keep them home. I knew I was going to have to go out as we had come to the end of our rice and I needed to make the fifteen-minute journey into town to buy another sack and some more food supplies. Once again, my thoughts were full of what ifs. What if the bandits returned? What if they had shot me – who would look after my children? What would happen to all the babies? What if Benjamin had pulled the trigger and shot himself? I felt frozen with fear and panic.

During the political instability, we never knew from this day to the next whether it was going to be possible to go out so I was always relieved when our storeroom had a good supply of food in it. On the Friday of that same week I found enough courage to take the children to school and make the short trip into town to buy a sack of rice and some dried food that would feed us for about a month. I bought my supplies at the shop and the shop boy packed them in the back of the car while I paid. As I walked out of the shop and came to unlock my car door, I just couldn't believe my eyes. There was a man there who accosted me. He had a grenade in his hand with his finger in the pin. He started making threats to me but I had no real idea of what he was saying. I was too tired and too exhausted to take any of it in. The events of the week quickly played themselves out in my mind: Hannah kidnapped, our wall blown up by a grenade, bandits threatening me at gunpoint, fearing Benjamin had been shot while I lay in the execution position – and now this! I assumed by his nervous gestures that he was telling me that if I didn't hand over my bag and money that he would pull the pin on the grenade. All of a sudden, I felt I had just had enough of the events of that week. I started yelling at the man and told him, "Just do it! Just pull the pin! See what happens, because me, I'm going to glory. If I die, I know where I'm going. Where do you think you're going? If you want to die, feel free. But for me, I know where I'm going." I pushed passed him, got into the car, still ranting and raving, and drove home. He was left standing there, looking embarrassed and not knowing what to do.

I could not believe what I had just done. Had I gone mad? I sat with a cup of coffee that one of the house girls made for me when I got home and recounted my story. It was crazy and I was relieved to have escaped death once again. All I could do at this point was to laugh and cry in equal measure.

The events of the week certainly had a profound effect on me. I wasn't sleeping at night and was afraid to let my children out of my sight. As I say, I hated going out but didn't feel safe staying in. The house was like Fort Knox with the new high wall and the new gate. But I realized that I was full of fear. I remembered that the antidote to fear is faith. I took time to search in my Bible and write out verses to do with fear. I discovered that there are 367 "fear not" verses in the Bible: one for every day of the year and an extra two for really bad days! Over a period of weeks, as I kept speaking out these verses and refusing to be paralysed by fear, I came to a place where I could clearly see that it was actually fear that had become my enemy – not the war, the thieves, the guns, or the child abductors. Fear of all these events bound me.

Early one morning, shortly after that dreadful week, God spoke to me very clearly from Psalm 23:5: "He has prepared before me a table in the presence of my enemies." It was as if God whispered in my ear, "Come and dine." I realized the table that He had set before me was the Word of God: my Bible. As I chose to take and believe all the truths that were written there; as I dined on all of those truths and embraced all of these verses, I acknowledged He is my refuge and my strength. He is a very present help in times of trouble and I need not fear. He is my protector.

He loves me. God's spirit is not a spirit of fear, but of peace, strength, and of a sound mind. How I needed to experience that afresh during the nights when I couldn't sleep and felt as if I were losing my mind. I made a choice to dine at the table of the Lord and not to allow fear to bind me any longer.

As I look back now, I see that it is possible to have fellowship with anything we choose to. By that, I mean that whatever we give room in our hearts to, whatever we embrace and think and talk about, the things we give our time to, our dreams and fears – they will grow only as we feed them and give them room. It is a good thing to learn to dine at the table of the King.

Since that particularly bad week, there have been other occasions when thieves have managed to get the better of me. It is sad, but it seems to be a part of life in Burundi, especially as so many people live with such poverty and deprivation. They sometimes have to steal in an attempt to stay alive and to keep their families alive. Desperate times produce desperate people.

Several years after this time, one of the men who had held me at gunpoint was sent to prison for a crime he committed afterwards. While serving his sentence he became a Christian and gave his life to the Lord. He sent for me to apologize and to ask for my forgiveness, and to tell me he was now saved and transformed. John 3:16 (NKJV) says "For God so loved the world that He gave His only begotten Son, that whoever believes in Him should not perish but have everlasting life." That was another truth to be embraced and my heart was thankful that this man had found this truth and was embracing it wholeheartedly.

CHAPTER 8

EMPTY THE STOREHOUSE

Since the beginning of the civil war when I felt called to help orphans and widows in particular, I have experienced a continual supernatural flow of provision. It seemed that no matter how much food we distributed, or how many people we fed, there was always enough. When we read Philippians 4:19 the apostle Paul says, "And my God will meet all your needs according to his glorious riches" (NIV), we think it is just referring to financial provision. I believe, however, it is so much more than that.

I do thank God for the people He has directed to help with the work in Burundi. We have had many local workers pass through our doors who unfortunately have ended up being more work for us, either through lack of commitment, stealing from us, or other such misdemeanours. But we have also had some of the most wonderful workers and collaborators: faithful people who have been a gift from God. They arrive with open hearts and a genuine desire to serve and have been such a huge part of God's provision in the lives of the children, and also for the many who just appeared as if from nowhere on our doorstep. It has been such a blessing to have dozens of expatriates, friends, and contacts who have come for various lengths of time from the UK, America, Canada, South Africa, Holland, and New Zealand – to mention but a few of the countries. What an amazing provision and blessing to have dear people come and give a few weeks, months, or even several years and to be willing to do whatever is asked of them in order to help.

At times I have felt as if I was walking up a steep hill laden with heavy shopping bags: struggling and feeling fatigued with the weight of the responsibility for so many on my shoulders. Then all of a sudden someone would arrive and take one of the bags from me and lighten my load. This is what happened time and time again as different folk came to help. They have lightened the load for a season, given a new lease of life with their love and servanthood, and have encouraged us to press on. Consequently, we have a fresh spring in our step, ready for the next lap. God's people certainly are God's provision.

Over the years I have also experienced favour from God in the shape of many donations coming our way. These have been donations of food, clothing, shoes, books, and school materials for the children. I will never forget how, many years ago, when we started feeding people who arrived at our home, a young man who was working as my administrator at the time applied to an organization here in the country called World Food Programme (WFP). They were distributing dried food to those in need. Our application was successful and we were issued with a couple of sacks of rice or maize flour and also some dried peas and beans. This provision was a real blessing each month for our babies who were growing quickly and needed more solid food – but also for our workers and for the many in need who turned up on our doorstep.

One day we had a visit from a young pastor. He told us he had just come from the border of Congo, which was only about eight to ten miles away from where we were living. He told us that there was a lot of unrest and fighting in Congo that had driven thousands of people from their homes and had resulted in many people congregating on the other side of the border. These poor people had had to quickly flee for their lives and so were often sick and hungry and had nothing other than the clothes they stood in. The young pastor said he thought there were probably about 2,000 people camped at the border and asked if we had anything at all we could donate to try and help them. As it happened, we had just received our monthly supply of dried food from the WFP. Without even thinking about it, I asked that our storehouse be emptied and all the food that we had in there be given to feed these dear people who were starving. Their need was so much greater than ours and, somehow, I just knew that God would not let us go hungry ourselves. As the food was being loaded into this pastor's truck, I felt God whisper in my ear, "Never eat your last sack of food. That is your seed!" How true that kingdom principle has proved to be: the multiplication is in the sowing. This action of giving somehow seemed to trigger a sort of chain reaction of blessing. We had a report back that when our donation was added to other small sacks given by others, the food that seemed so small in quantity, just seemed to multiply when it was cooked. There was enough to feed everybody.

When we explained to the WFP that we had given all our food away, they gave us more! This time, however, we received about ten times as much and that provision continued for a whole year – for as long as the contract lasted. We were so blessed with all that food. We were able to help hundreds of people, especially widows and orphans. We also started to feed street children who gathered in the church compound. We either gave them *ubuyi* or sometimes a hot meal. At the same time, we were able to look out for those who were in need of medical treatment so that we could refer them to one of the other African Revival Ministries' clinics.

There was also a large number of women with their babies at the AIDS clinic. All of them were desperately poor. Those mothers taking medication were not allowed to breastfeed. Somehow, God provided and enabled us to buy fresh milk for all the babies and we donated sacks of dried food to the medical team at the clinic so that they could distribute it among the needy. Over and over, we continually received such provision of food and finances to be able to help hundreds of people.

Back at home the children were all growing up. We had managed to buy two of the five houses we were using (we bought the second house in the early 2000s), and we rented the other three. The owner of House 2 had a very large plot of land adjoining it. This land already had the foundations of another house being built on it but it looked quite derelict and the land was very overgrown. Our workers decided to use that land to grow some crops as it was not being used for anything else. They had the most amazing harvest of maize followed by a huge harvest of groundnuts. It became clear that what we needed was a purpose-built building: a centre for the children where they could be housed on the same compound. The cost of renting, combined with high running costs, salaries for the workers, and of course food was proving to be prohibitive. It was very difficult for me to keep a close eye on everything that was happening with the children spread between five houses. We started to feel very overstretched. It was time for a new plan.

This dream for a purpose-built centre where we could have all the children living on the same compound was one that I'd had for a long time. It made sense from the point of view of supervision, cost, and security to have everyone close together. I was convinced this was a God idea and not just a good idea. After experiencing such an outpouring of provision over the years, I knew that if this was in God's plan, He would provide the funds to get it built.

The first thing to do was to find an architect to draw up some plans for a building. I was very sure that we needed a building that would not feel like an institution: definitely no dormitory-type bedrooms. I felt it was also important to keep the children in small family groups. Thinking of the future, it was also important that living quarters for the boys and girls were separate as the children grew into teenagers and young adults.

After a lot of thought, prayer, and planning, we came up with a draft plan for a two-storey building which would be divided into four four-bedroom apartments. Each one would have two bathrooms, a sitting room, a small kitchen, and a small storeroom. The main kitchen, as is normal in Africa, would be built outside, and was where the food would be cooked for everyone in one place. Running the whole length of the front of the building, a large balcony would be constructed where all the children could eat together. There would be a door at each end of the building so boys and girls could enter the house separately. There was also enough space to build a small block of rooms at the back with showers for the workers. We could also build a reasonably sized staff house. In fact, before any of the building work started, it was decided that this house would be for Rosa, her husband Deo, and their children; Rosa and Deo would eventually be the couple who would have the main oversight for both the children and the workers on a day-to-day basis.

Rosa and Deo were by this time more like part of my family than employees. Deo had been with me since I arrived in the country, first as my guard at the clinic, then as my cook. After some years, he had fallen in love with Rosa and they married. We had then set up our third rented house and they started married life with ten of the orphaned children! Deo learned to drive and very quickly became the much-needed driver for all the shopping and running around: such a blessing as the work continued to grow and life seemed to get busier and busier.

The plans were completed in no time at all, and with the small amount of money we had in the bank already, work began. Because the building was two-storey, the foundations needed to be very deep. To get the foundations laid for the first building was a real step of faith. We had approximately $20,000 to get started, knowing that somehow we needed about $250,000 for the entire project. There was enough to begin the project while trusting and praying for the rest of the finance to come in.

The building of the CRIB centre was one of the most exciting and challenging adventures I have experienced. Every time money was needed to continue onto the next phase, it appeared. When I look back, I am still amazed at how all the money came in at exactly the time we needed it. We had donations from individuals and church groups from all over the world. I will never forget the day when the cement was laid for the second floor. It had to be started and finished in one go, without a pause. A huge team of workmen began preparing and mixing the cement early in the morning; it was not until early evening that they finally started to pour the cement into place. With the aid of floodlights they laboured all night until it was complete.

With a huge cheer of relief, they celebrated by barbecuing a couple of goats and had the most wonderful feast – what a night to remember that was. The walls went up in no time once the second storey was begun. Very soon, they were approaching the last phase: the roof. I couldn't believe how far we had come. We started making lists of all the equipment we needed to buy to furnish the centre.

On completion of the building, we needed new bunk beds as the children's beds and cots were now getting too small for them. Mattresses, bedding, sitting-room furniture – the list got longer and longer and the amount of things we needed seemed endless. But God had got us this far and there was no going back; the only way was forward. Bear in mind that for all the months the CRIB centre was being built, we were still paying rent for all the other houses and shouldering the considerable running costs. What a mighty God we serve – every week, every bill was paid on time.

It was now August 2006 and the day finally came when the new centre was completed. The grounds still looked like a building site but once the outside kitchen was built and the workers' rooms finished, we decided that one group of children at a time would move in over a period of a few days. Once again we were overwhelmed and overjoyed as money poured in, enabling us to buy all the beds, mattresses, and furniture we needed, as well as new kitchen equipment. We chose material and had curtains made for all the bedrooms and sitting rooms and the place started to look homely and welcoming.

By the time the children moved in with all their own little possessions, it became home very quickly. With the slightly older girls upstairs on one side of the house and the younger ones downstairs and the same on the other side for the boys, we had approximately sixteen children upstairs on each side and twelve downstairs, and a house mother in each apartment to supervise. With mostly even numbers of boys and girls it worked well and it proved to be really good to operate as four separate apartments.

Along with the great blessings of this time, there was also the great challenge of having over fifty children all living in the same building. In the years that lay ahead, we rode the storms of the teenage years together and it felt like "hormone city" for a while!

With the children all moved in and enjoying the adventure of living together in the same compound, work started once again. We used the small amount of money left over in the bank account to build Rosa and Deo and their their children a new house. For the time being, Rosa and Deo stayed living in the last of the small houses we had rented. It wasn't far from the CRIB house but not at all easy for Rosa having to move in between the two every day because of needing to supervise the staff with their new work routines. Added to this, some of the children took longer to settle into their new lives with so many other children and workers around all of the time. Once again, God provided in the most amazing way. In just eight months the house for Rosa and Deo was completed and ready for them to move into. What a blessing to walk around those houses and grounds as new grass was planted and to see the wonderful new play area with brightly coloured climbing frames and all manner of play equipment for the children to play on. It was a miracle constructed of bricks and mortar and it was amazing to see how God had opened the floodgates of provision to enable all this to happen. What a blessing!

I have learned a lot over the years about faith and destiny and in many ways I think they go hand in hand like a pair of gloves. I have had the privilege of being around people who were giants in God when it came to living by faith. Bob and Hilda Gordon were such people. Bob was the director of Roffey Place and it was he who first brought me to Burundi to help pray for the sick. This was the first time I had really ever seen faith in action in such a huge way. I had never heard anyone with such a gift of teaching from the Scriptures – he had such a depth of understanding and such revelation and anointing and the ability to bring the word of God to life. I saw great miracles of provision time and time again as we prayed and believed for all kinds of financial need including vehicles and buildings. I saw that faith was not just wishful thinking. Faith is the evidence of things hoped for. This hope is not just a wish or a good idea – it is a revelation that comes from the Holy Spirit that with God all things are possible if we only believe, and faith is the result of embracing that truth and not letting go of it.

David and Ruth Ndaruhutse were another couple who exhibited great faith. I met David the first time I came to Burundi with Bob Gordon on the two-week placement, and worked under his leadership a few years later. He was another giant when it came to living by faith. I can see so clearly why the Lord put me beside these people: to learn from them as a preparation for when I came to live and work in this little war-torn African country.

Faith is not something you can really learn from a book. It is something that occurs when you are around people who live in an attitude of expectancy. When you spend time with people who believe that all things are possible and believe God can do the impossible, it is hard not to be affected by this. Life will never be the same again as you find yourself moving onward and forward and not giving up until God shows up. Faith is contagious but you have to be willing to catch it and for it to change you. People of great faith provoke you to reach out to God in ways you never think are possible. They magnify Jesus so that you want to change and be more like Jesus.

In Burundi the war continued but there was also a lot of unrest and fighting in the neighbouring countries of Rwanda and Congo. Although Burundi was still in turmoil, the fleeing of people from their homes was not such an issue now. Those who still had homes standing started to repair them and plant crops again. There were thousands in the camps for displaced people who had no way of returning to their destroyed homes. They could only rely on help from the various agencies who were at work in the country and who had the massive task of trying to repatriate such large numbers of people.

As the months passed all our children became well settled and had mostly come through their traumatic experiences. I began to feel it would not be right to add any more children to our centre but rather to be able to support those who came to our door by placing them either with a relative or a friend. We would support the whole family and keep the baby or child out in the community. This in fact worked well. The situation was still not good in the country but things were improving and there was not the widespread abandonment of babies when people fled for their lives as there once had been. As the needs were now different we changed our strategy accordingly.

However, one morning in August 2004, we received news that a group of people from Congo who had fled over the Burundi border and set up a small camp, had been attacked. Many of the men had been killed and some of the women too. There was a small number of surviving women and children. One of the pastors who came from the church had taken all the survivors to his home. There were over twenty children and their mothers and other relatives as well. They were all deeply traumatized and some of them were injured. We tried to help out by taking in a couple of the very small babies but it would have been too much for our CRIB children and also for these traumatized Congolese children to pack them into our house. Once again, we talked together and decided that the best plan was to rent a large house or homes that would be big enough to house them all. I, and Pastors Ray and Mary Anne Bale, alerted all our prayer partners to ask for help to raise funds. Our intention was to pay three months rent on a large house which we were yet to find.

What happened was beyond my wildest dreams: once again people responded in obedience and we received enough money to actually buy a property. In fact, what became available was a whole compound with several small houses. It took time to get the funds transferred and to process the purchase of the land. The buildings did need a lot of repair and redecoration and once again supplies were needed to furnish the houses and get them into a liveable state. It happened nonetheless. All the money that was needed came in and The New Hope Centre, like CRIB, has continued to house orphaned children since its establishment in 2005, and many more children have been added to their number. Our vision is the same: to raise these children to be young men and women who know that God has saved and rescued them because He has a plan for their lives – for them to make a difference in Burundi.

It never ceases to amaze me that over the years all the people who have come to join us and work as part of our team, always seem to be the right people at the right time. One family who came to join us, Fred and Else Marie Regier from Niagara Falls in Canada, came and served with us for two years with their four children. Fred is a carpenter and did a wonderful job making bunk beds for the baby unit. Else Marie is a nurse and worked wonders with the malnourished and poorly babies who were in the baby unit. One of our babies, Alida, contracted cerebral meningitis and almost died. Having survived, she is now severely brain damaged. As far as we can tell, she is both deaf and blind and paralysed from the neck down. In the very early days Alida needed a lot of nursing care. What a gift to have another trained nurse on the team. Now nearly fourteen years of age, the Lord has not healed her so far but she has survived numerous infections and it is a mystery to the medical staff how she can swallow. They say she shouldn't be able to eat but she does and she keeps going. She has one Mama now who has the responsibility to care for her and we continue to pray and know that either one day she will be healed on earth or else receive a new body from Jesus in heaven. Some of these things we do not understand fully but our part is to trust and believe that Jesus is Lord in the situations we cannot fathom.

God connects people and uses situations and circumstances that at the time seem so difficult. I remember the time I was taking a short holiday in England with my children and while we were out of the country, there was an embargo and all flights were stopped as the borders were closed. We were stranded. It seemed to be a disastrous situation, but somehow in a way only God can, I was introduced to Barney Coombs who at that time headed up the Salt & Light group of churches in the UK and across

Canada. As well as being invited to speak at their summer camp in the UK, I was also invited to go to Canada to speak at some of the churches there, which, as I have mentioned before, is where I met Ray and Mary Anne Bale who brought out that wonderful Salt & Light team to build the baby unit in the garden of the main house. I also went to Winnipeg where I met the most wonderful folk, some of whom also came to Burundi to help. Hannah, my daughter, spent two years in school in Winnipeg and graduated there enabling her to go to university in London. Only God can work out these divine connections. All such a big part of God's provision. We were so thankful for people with the skills to help us who achieved so much for us.

Another situation that at the time left me feeling devastated was when I found a lump in one of my breasts and had to fly back to the UK for further investigations. In fact I was diagnosed with cancer in both breasts. I had to have a bilateral mastectomy. The end result was good and I have been cancer-free for thirteen years now. However, between 2002 and 2003 I had to take a year out. My children and I stayed in the UK in a house that my home church very kindly rented for us. I home-schooled Ben, Hannah, and Lydia while I was having treatment but I was prompted at that time to apply to adopt my children through the UK courts and thus give them British citizenship. This was granted and would save me many trips to Uganda (our nearest British embassy) to get the visas needed for the children to be able to travel with me. Again God's favour was on us. It seemed that in record time the adoptions were processed and completed.

If I had not undergone that surgery, I probably would never have taken a year out in the UK. The adoptions probably would never have been processed and now, years later, I cannot understand why it had to happen that way but I am thankful that it did and so blessed that my children have been able to travel to so many places all over the world without all the issues, problems, and expense of obtaining visas for these various places. At the age of sixteen Lydia left school in Burundi and went to the UK. For two years she stayed in Taunton, Somerset, to attend a hairdressing college. She has since travelled to many places in Canada and did a Discipleship Training School (DST) course for Youth With A Mission (YWAM) in America. She then worked with a team that worked in Mexico, India, and then Nepal. Hannah attended high school in Canada for two years before starting at a university in London to study law and history. Benjamin, meanwhile, attended college and university in the UK and studied music and production. Who except God could possibly have seen so far ahead, knowing what needed to be done to enable my children to fulfil the plans God had for their lives?

Some of my closest and dearest friendships have come about as a result of what first started out as a catastrophe or a mistake. I met my dear friends in Santa Barbara because David Ndaruhutse double-booked two teams who arrived from different states in the USA. David couldn't spread himself to supervise both teams so I stepped in to help out with the team of five who came from Santa Barbara. As a result, divine connections and friendships were formed and have lasted for years. Three of our children, Nizi, Abel, and Ciza were adopted by a pastor, Dale, and his wife, Amy, from Santa Barbara.

My life has been like a beautiful rich tapestry that only God could put together. I am continually overwhelmed by the people with whom God connects me: strangers who have opened up their homes and their hearts and offered accommodation to me and a place to rest when I am in the UK; when I am travelling, strangers who have become friends within hours – kindred spirits, encouragers – and I am blessed beyond measure with the family of God.

After that bad week in September 1995 when I was held at gunpoint (to name just one of the incidents), David Ndarahutse came to visit me and told me that he was booked to go to South Africa to speak at a Newfrontiers conference. He invited me to go with him. He thought the small break and a change of scenery would do me good. After chatting with my household, I decided that because I was still feeling rather frayed around the edges, it seemed like a good idea to go. Rosa was more than willing to keep things going while I was away.

When we arrived in South Africa, I was introduced to a couple called Terry and Wendy Virgo. Terry, along with David, was the main speaker. Once again, this was a divine connection. God seemed to put His stamp of blessing on our friendship, and after a few days it felt as if we had been close friends for years.

I returned to Burundi feeling blessed, encouraged and refreshed. A short time later I received an email invitation to go to the Newfrontiers summer camp back in the UK in Stoneleigh, Warwickshire, together with my family. We went and returned the following year as well. I was given the opportunity to share some testimony and to speak with Wendy in the women's meetings. These were divine opportunities and connections and some of the people I met at those camps, as had happened at other events, came out to Burundi to join the team and help with the work of CRIB. Some of them enabled us to move forward in the next phase of what God was calling us to do – to start our own school. This was a challenge that I thought would take me too far out of my depth, but then I remembered: *nothing is impossible with God!*

CHAPTER 9

THE KING'S SCHOOL

Never in my wildest dreams could I have imagined that God could use someone like me to start a school. I was never a shining star at school myself; I just about managed to maintain average grades. I came from a loving working-class family and none of us had very high expectations of life. The goal was to get through school, find a job, earn a wage, and survive. My first job was in a shirt factory sitting at a machine sewing buttons on shirts – not the kind of work that was going to hold my attention for long. I had no idea what life had in store for me but I knew that there had to be more to life than sitting sewing in a factory.

Up to this point, my life had been like a roller coaster with many ups and downs but I did manage to press on and somehow fulfil my dream to train as a registered nurse and midwife. Through a whole series of events and life experiences, as mentioned before, I eventually ended up at Roffey Place before being called to Burundi. Many of my friends and colleagues along life's journey would probably say I was the most unlikely person to go to Africa as a missionary. However, I thank God that once I put myself, with all of my flaws and weaknesses, into His hands, I seemed to be the person God needed in Burundi. I said yes and the rest was up to Him.

The idea of starting a school began after the horrendous experience we had had with Hannah's abduction back in 1995. After that incident, I never really felt that my children were completely safe when they were in school. The continuing unrest in the country also didn't help. I always encouraged my workers to listen to the local radio station so they could alert me to any trouble in our vicinity. I could then get to the school immediately and bring the children home safely.

At this time, I began thinking about having a small room built at the side of the house that would work as a schoolroom. I could look for a teacher who would come out and take on the task of home-schooling my children. I duly arranged for local builders to construct a small schoolroom and planned to look for a teacher when I was back in the UK on my summer holiday. At the time, in 1997, Benjamin was three, Hannah nearly five, and Lydia eight. However, as usual our plans took a detour and during the period the room was being built we unexpectedly had some slightly older children along with their baby siblings come to join the CRIB family. So now, sooner than I thought, I had to begin to make plans for the babies and children I had taken in. Obviously, some of the older children would need to be provided with an education. The truth is, I had been so busy trying to rescue the babies and save them from certain death that I never thought through what I was going to do in the long term. Once I started to think about the future and the huge responsibility I now had with all these lives in my care, I started to feel a little panic stricken. It was no longer possible just to think about my own little family. At that time, I had another seventeen babies under a year old in every bit of space in my house and four children aged between three and eight. What was I going to do?

Somewhere in the midst of all the thinking and praying, God led me to Libby and Annelie who came out to Burundi to help us. Then as we were able to build the baby unit, rent another house, and share out the responsibility of the children, life became a bit easier. As we talked and prayed, we did indeed decide to look for a teacher from the UK to come out and start a small school for our children. This teacher would come to teach all the children in our care, not just my three children. We felt this teacher would need to speak and teach in French as French was the language used in most schools in Burundi.

During that summer break in 1997, I was at one of the Newfrontiers camps in the UK and met Angela, a teacher who could speak and teach in French and who had a desire to come to Burundi and help us. Plans were made. I returned to Africa and located a small house opposite our dwelling with a huge lounge that could be used as a schoolroom. This house would be perfect for Angela to live in. With great anticipation and excitement, we welcomed

Angela, our first teacher, and our little school consisting of only eight children was born in her front room. The small schoolroom I had had built in my garden at the side of my house never did get used as a schoolroom. It has, instead, made a fantastic and much needed store room for sacks of food over the years!

Things went well with the children's learning and they were well occupied all morning. As the year went on, it became clear that we could not just keep adding more and more children to the little schoolroom when they reached the age of three. Also, with the varying age range and maturity levels of the children, Angela was finding the task of teaching all of them an understandable challenge. Adding more small children into this mix just would not work. It was clear that we would have to rethink and re-plan. We decided to take a week to pray and fast and seek God for wisdom and direction to know what we should do. We still felt very sure that we should not put these children into the public school system. Quite apart from trying to get them all placed in the same school and the expense and logistics of taking care of each of their travel arrangements every day, some of the children were still working through a lot of trauma.

As we met together to talk and pray every day for that week, we came to the conclusion that it was right to start a proper school. We would need to find a building we could rent with rooms big enough to be used as classrooms. We needed other teachers, maybe two or three, so we could divide the children into age groups. The other thing we decided was that this school should be English-speaking. We were about to embark on starting the first Christian English-speaking school in Burundi. I was clear that this was what God was telling us to do but I also had more questions than answers at that point in time (especially about the English-speaking bit!). But I was also excited and ready for action. However, I am not a teacher and didn't have any contacts in the teaching profession whom I could ask for either help or advice. For now, we kept praying that God would locate the right building and the right teachers for us.

I decided to leave Lydia and Hannah in the school they already attended to give Angela time to adjust with as few children as possible to start with. I also didn't want to make too many changes too soon for Lydia and Hannah. Ben was still too young for nursery school. It was as I was walking to school with them one morning that I passed a large house on a corner with a lot of building work going on in the grounds. I decided to walk inside the gate and have a look. I was amazed at the size of the compound. As I walked round the place I could see that they were building a large open-plan area with an attractive zigzag design on the roof. The building ran the whole length of the outside perimeter wall and the whole length of the side walls backing onto the neighbouring property. There were several supporting structural posts but nothing else. As I stood there, I started to imagine what it would look like with some dividing walls that would create classrooms but would also keep it as open plan as possible. Would it work just to build half walls at the front? I calculated that we could easily get five or six good-sized classrooms. This surely would be all we needed and more to educate my orphan children! The large four-bedroom house in the centre would work well as accommodation for the teachers. It had two bedrooms on each side of a large sitting room with a bathroom on either side and another small sitting room with yet another room off that. I was walking round and planning it in my head. One small area could be a sitting room for the teachers, the room next to it, a storeroom. I envisaged a larger area as maybe an assembly room. I was so excited but did not know if this property was actually available to rent! I could hardly contain myself and couldn't wait to get home and tell Libby and Annelie about this amazing discovery.

We managed to get an appointment to talk to the owner of the house. It transpired he had a plan to rent the building. In his mind, he had thought it would make a great restaurant. The large open plan area would be filled with tables and chairs where customers could dine. A good plan, but I doubted it would ever have been successful in this quiet area, which was quite a distance from the city. So far from the city, not many people ventured out in the evenings for meals. As we talked, I began to share my own thoughts and vision for our school, asking about the possibility of building internal walls to make classrooms. Within a week a contract was drawn up for the rental, which I had to sign before the owner was willing to instruct the builders to make this proposed restaurant into a school. The rent was going to be $1,000 a month. Now I just needed to find the funds and the teachers!

As I look back at this period, it is so clear how God allowed a number of events to take place that caused doors to open allowing me to connect with different folk, especially at some of the summer camps in the UK that drew several thousands of people every year. It was mostly through meeting people at the Salt & Light camp in Harrogate, Yorkshire, and the Newfrontiers camp at Stoneleigh that I met teachers and other young people who were interested and willing to come out and help. We were not in a position to pay any of them a salary so it was necessary for those who came to get the financial backing, support, and approval from their own churches. I will be forever grateful to all those teachers and gap-year students who came out in those early years to sow into the lives of our children, whether in a teaching capacity or just to cuddle the babies and play with the toddlers. I am so thankful to the churches who gave their support to those who came out to assist us. There have been so many who have given so much. Most of the teachers in those early years came for a relatively short time: some for a year and a few for two years. It was a challenge every year to find new teachers, not just to replace those who left, but every year the school was growing and another year group was added to our number.

We finally opened in 1998 and it wasn't too long before people came enquiring about places for their children. At first I resisted all such enquiries and was adamant that this school was going to be just for the CRIB children. As time went on, however, and more and more people came knocking at the door, I began to feel that this might be a real blessing. It was a private Christian school. We had teachers with relatively small numbers of children in their classes. Why not open the doors to other children? We were using a British curriculum and planned to start teaching French and Kirundi in language classes. We had a lot of help and advice from contacts at the King's School in Oxford, UK: people who had wisdom and experience in how to start a Christian school and were willing to come and train our teachers in Christian education. It also seemed good to mix with children from other nationalities outside of our compound. It was therefore decided to open our doors to the general public with the proviso that they accepted our terms and values. School fees would be charged – the fees would help to cover the cost of the monthly rent and all the books and equipment that we needed.

As the numbers increased, the expenses multiplied, and even though we were not paying our expatriate teachers a salary, we did add a number of local teachers to the school team whom we did pay. For quite a number of years, CRIB still had to cover a lot of the extra costs of the school not covered by the fee-paying students. It didn't matter to us as the school was never a money-making project; the vision was to educate and to raise young men and women who would make a difference wherever life took them. The vision of the school was to introduce all who attended to Jesus and to send them out with a good education. Our school motto was "Excellence is not an option".

As our doors opened to other students, so God directed us to other teachers. We needed those who fully embraced the vision of the school and, most importantly, teachers with a background of education who would be willing to head up our team of teachers. We also needed to get some stability by employing teachers who stayed for more than just a year or two. Opening up the school had huge ramifications.

It seemed that all of a sudden the whole project snowballed. Just as my house had seemed so large before CRIB began with the arrival of seventeen babies, and then quickly seemed to shrink in size, it was the same with the school building. I had moved very quickly from feeling that this building was going to be all that we would ever need to thinking, "What are we going to do next?" We had actually run out of classroom space!

There was no going back. We had to grow with the need. We would need some extra building work to alter selected storage space and create another large classroom. A new toilet block also had to be built and, in time, as more teachers and further classes were added, the main house was no longer used to accommodate teachers. We now needed an office, a storeroom, and a library. New houses had to be found and rented for our teachers to live in in the surrounding area. With Burundi still politically unstable, the houses we rented needed to be within walking distance of the school (and of each other).

Of course, the time had now come to sit down and talk with the landlord about buying the school.

It has been my experience over the years that the Lord has a variety of ways of doing things and it was important for me to get some clear wisdom from God at this time. If it really was Him prompting me to buy this school, He would show me how to go about it. However, we didn't have great reserves of cash just waiting to be spent. With the building of the CRIB centre, I felt it was right to start building with the small amount of money we had in the bank. However, US $20,000 was not so little, as long as we didn't sit too long and think about the other $230,000 we needed to complete the CRIB centre. This time it was different. The owner was willing to sell and the price was agreed but I needed to know how to complete the deal. There was only one thing left to do and that was to go back to the prayer closet and ask God for wisdom and clarity that this really was the way forward. Provision of the finances would also be very welcome too!

Well, God didn't let me down. Within a very short period of time, the pastor from my home church in the UK phoned me to say that they had some money in a building fund they wanted to donate to us. It amounted to approximately 60 per cent of what was needed. I felt that I could now go and offer this money as a down payment and the rest would be paid in monthly instalments over a period of ten to twelve months. This agreement was acceptable to the owner and approximately a year later the school was bought and owned under the African Revival Ministries charity. With a headteacher now on board, a full quota of classes from the nursery and infants right up until the end of primary, the time had now come to look for a suitable building to rent as a secondary school. I felt excited but the daunting nature of the task made me feel weak at the knees. Of course, by now my own three children as well as about thirty of the other children were all students of the King's School and loving it. Once again it was important to try and find a building within walking distance for our children, and if possible, as close to the primary school as possible. Again, we found exactly the right building: a two-storey house with large rooms suitable for classrooms and huge grounds for a playground and sports area. Rent and contract once again were arranged and some work was done in one of the downstairs rooms to convert it into a small science laboratory. In six short years we had moved from eight children in the front room of Angela's house to a full school, incorporating nursery through to Year 6 primary with about fifteen students in each class, and now a secondary school was added, which was about a five minute walk away.

I wonder if the day will ever come when I stop feeling completely amazed at what God does: the way He leads and goes before us every step of the way. I know I should not be amazed, but I am. For reasons I still do not understand, I was the one God chose to give the vision to start the school. Well, I always knew the most important part of any vision is to have the right people in the right places, and this is particularly true of the school. We had been so blessed with the teachers the Lord had brought out to us.

Life continued and the school added a new class every year. Teachers came from the UK, the USA, Canada, and New Zealand to work with us. We also had three national teachers and the time came when we started to bring teachers from other English-speaking African countries, including Kenya and Uganda. As we were moving toward the students taking the International General Certificate of Secondary Education (IGCSE) exams, there was now the whole process of getting the school registered with the government and the National Board of Examiners. Once again, God brought the right people at the right time in every area – not just teachers but also administrators who did all the tedious paperwork to make sure everything was legal and in order. We added a full-time accountant as the members of staff and school workers continued to grow. We now needed to start thinking about writing such things as school policies as time went on and things progressed.

The time had come for us to find a principal – someone who would fully embrace our vision for Christian education. The person we were seeking would also have the gifting and leadership ability to take the school forward: to bring the school to a place of excellence in every area; to continue what had been started but to go even further. I asked myself, was there such a person? Yes, indeed, once again I found myself visiting friends in Canada. I was with Ray and Mary Anne Bale who were now pastoring a church in Vernon, British Columbia. Because of his previous work in Burundi, Ray had a real heart for our work with the orphans, the school, and everything else that we were involved in. As we talked together and prayed, I knew that Ray and Mary Anne felt the great weight of the burden I was carrying for the school – and my feelings of inadequacy. God spoke to them to come to Burundi again to support us, doing whatever their hands found to do. Once again, I was amazed and completely overwhelmed at the Lord's love and goodness, and the love and care of this wonderful couple who were willing to sell their home, leave their married daughters and grandchildren, and pack up to come and work alongside us in this little African country.

Ray stepped in and took up the role of principal in the school. His leadership and pastoral gifting was so evident as the school team blossomed under his leadership and encouragement. As we met together with a small team each week, it was clear that a couple who had been with us for some time, David and Debbie, should be given the position of head teachers since the previous incumbent had returned to the UK. She had been teaching in the school almost since it started and had met David when he came out from Kenya to teach in the secondary school, and they subsequently got married. They were both tremendously committed to the school. Now Debbie was officially appointed as head of primary and David as head of secondary. From then on, it was onward and upwards! The school was successfully registered and the first ever IGCSE exams to take place in Burundi occurred at the King's School. Wow! I never imagined I would see this day! One of the proudest days of my life was the day I was invited to give some words of encouragement to that first group of students on their graduation day.

Most of those young graduates had been in the school since its inception and among them was Lydia, the elder of my two daughters. As I looked into the faces of all the students in the school, it was one of the most emotional and humbling of experiences. All these lives had been blessed by being part of something started because God had a plan for these orphan children to be educated. The blessing was truly overflowing. As I sat with my head in my hands when everyone else had left the building, I could only say once again that only God had got us this far and only God could get us to where we needed to be next.

Since the time the school started, many changes have occurred in Burundi. One of those changes has been the introduction of English as the official second language in most of the schools across the country. There are now several other English-speaking schools and as Burundi became part of the East African Community, this pushed our school into being the forerunner of English education in the country. Places in the school were very much in demand for expatriates as well as for nationals.

The school has also developed rapidly over time. It has grown considerably, with demand for more student places, more classes, and A-level education added. I felt very much that a tidal wave had indeed swept the school forward with more buildings, more teachers, and more students. Those with strong leadership qualities and experience have taken the reins of the school and pushed it forward. Now, with hundreds of students over four different sites and dozens of teachers and classroom assistants and a whole group of administration staff, our little mission school is now a large international school preparing children to be educated, equipped, and envisioned.

Pastor Ray and I are no longer involved with the day-to-day activities of the school. Ray and Mary Anne are now working with the pastor who oversees the New Hope Orphanage, which takes in children from the Congo. Those children are now being educated at the King's School.

CRIB still has over thirty children in the school, several have graduated and gone on to university in other countries. Some have found work here in Burundi. In the summer of 2015, nine of our children will graduate, two from the A-level courses and another seven after completing the IGCSE exams. We have no more children in the primary school – all of our children from the CRIB centre that are still at school are in the secondary school. In approximately five to six years' time, every one of the children in our care at the CRIB home will have completed their education at the King's School.

Our children have developed into young men and women who will go on to reach for their own dreams. Some will go to universities in different countries, others to colleges, others will learn a trade. It is an awesome privilege to have been chosen by God to share in the destiny of this group of young people; to have been a part of them growing up, to have seen them loved and cared for, to have been able to offer them the very best education that money could buy, and to stand at the end of this journey with young men and women who are whole, healed, educated, and confident has been wonderful. The greatest blessing, however, is to see them loving Jesus and knowing it is Jesus who has made all this possible for them.

The school will go on from strength to strength. People will come and go – that is the nature of such a project. This King's School will always have a very special place in my heart. The seed was planted there by the Holy Spirit. This is truly evidence that God can use anyone who is willing to say yes to his prompting. He takes our inadequacies and if we are willing to do what we can with what we have, He will do the rest.

My work these days is mainly in finding ways to help these young people to reach their goals and do whatever I can as we are now coming to the last lap of this most incredible journey. The future will continue to be a walk of faith, trusting God for all the finances needed to get all these young people to the end of their education and to a place where they will be able to be independent and working to support themselves. Wow, what a day that will be.

I have come such a long way from sewing buttons on shirts in a factory to being the Mama of fifty-three wonderful children. What a long way these children have come, snatched from certain death during a brutal civil war to a place of knowing they are children of the King. Their destiny is not determined by where they came from or what happened to their families. Their destiny is determined by who they are now and the choices that they make for tomorrow. It is such a joy for those of us who have had a part in the lives of these young people, not just to see a group of orphans but to look into the faces of young men and women who have embraced the truth that Jesus is Lord and who have embraced the truth that Jesus has spared them and saved them because He has a plan for their lives.

CHAPTER 10

THE NEXT GENERATION

Over twenty years have passed since the arrival of my first rescued baby and the work of CRIB began in earnest. We are now navigating life with those babies who have grown into fine young people. For many of them, the last lap of their CRIB journey is upon them. Some have already graduated from school and many others will very soon follow in their footsteps. It is a time to look forward and to make plans and decisions about the next stage in the journey. What does life look like after CRIB?

When the children were young people they would often ask me what I was going to do with them when they grew up. Where would they go? For me, it was never really an issue. I am their Mama. What does a mother do when her children grow up? It has never been a question of what to do, more how to do it. Not many families have nine children graduating from school at the same time, but that is exactly what is about to happen quite soon in our CRIB family.

Every one of these youngsters has a dream for their life

and it is our plan to do what we can to direct, guide, and help each of these children to reach their potential. For some who have academic ability, the plan is to go on to university. We will help them to find a suitable establishment (whether in Burundi or in another country) and trust God once again to open the floodgates and provide the finance needed to pay their fees and expenses. For those with more practical skills, we will search for situations where their skills can be developed so that they can support themselves and be financially independent.

This book is written primarily for the CRIB children – the children who have been rescued in Burundi. In total, we have fifty children raised in the care of the CRIB home: twenty-seven boys and twenty-three girls. If I also add the three children I adopted: Lydia, Hannah and Ben that makes me the proud Mama of fifty-three children! Each of them was spared death and survived because God had a plan for them. Each one deserves a mention in this chapter for they are beginning a new season of life, moving from the CRIB home and entering the world of work.

Of course, there are dozens who didn't make it and were with us for a very short time, some for just a matter of hours, and others days or weeks, too weak or sick to survive. There are hundreds more whom we have reached out to with food or medical treatment, or supported them and their extended families in the community. Some of these youngsters I have mentioned in earlier chapters, but for all of them their stories are worth telling and their lives worth talking about because they are survivors – born and saved for such a day as this.

The Boys

Gentil came to us when he was seven years old; he had no surviving family. He has a real passion for agriculture. He finished school and completed a one-year agricultural course in Uganda called Farming God's Way. Currently Gentil is working in The King's School as a classroom assistant. He is diligently saving his money so that one day he can rent or buy his own piece of land and grow his own crops. He dreams of being independent, having his own family, and of living life to the full.

Murungwa came to CRIB at the age of eight, after his mother and baby brother died in hospital. He settled in and did very well in school, and this year he will graduate from university in Uganda with a degree in Computer Sciences. He would love to return to Burundi and start his own IT business. I have absolutely no doubt that in this he will succeed.

Budusy was six or seven years old when he came to CRIB. I remember that he was the size of a two-year-old when he arrived and had no surviving relatives. He is currently attending university in Kenya and is halfway through his degree in Computer Technology. He was one of the most traumatized children we took in. It is a miracle to see him now: a young man with vision and purpose.

Moise (formerly Ngabire) was the little boy found abandoned on the doorstep of the Catholic church. He was taken to a refugee camp and cared for by a local lady who had several children of her own. The extra mouth to feed proved to be too much for this lady so we at CRIB took him in. He was then adopted by a lady from the church who later died from tuberculosis. He again returned to CRIB but this time for good. He has done well at school and is currently studying at university in Oklahoma, USA. His dream is to be a civil engineer and I have every confidence that he will succeed in this.

David arrived when he was a few days old and had no relatives we could trace. He had a rocky childhood with almost continual chronic ear infections. David loves sport and has graduated from school. He now works as an assistant sports teacher at The King's School.

Keve came to CRIB when he was about three or four years of age. He has a mother and siblings but a rather complicated family situation. Keve graduated from school and has worked as an IT classroom assistant in our primary school. He is about to go to college in the USA for two years for further training in computer technology and business studies.

We took **Enoch** when he was about twenty months old. His parents, brothers, and sisters were all killed in the war. It was a miracle that Enoch survived. He has a large gash on his elbow where he was hit with a machete during the attack that killed his mother. Enoch is now nineteen years old and about to complete his A levels. He is also preparing to go to the USA with Keve to attend the same college. Enoch has a plan to be a construction manager. His heart has been moved over the last few years by the devastation of so many homes in Burundi, wrecked by the heavy rains, which has left hundreds of people homeless. Once he gains the right training and skills, I know he will return to Burundi and make a real difference in his community.

Pacifique came to CRIB when he was two or three years old. He was found under a tree in someone's garden. Pacifique is in his first year at university in Burundi studying hotel management and tourism and is doing well.

Samuel arrived the same day as David and was also only a few days old. His mother had died after giving birth to him and no other known relatives were found. Samuel will complete his A levels this year and is looking at universities. He would like to be a journalist and dreams of one day being an author.

Ezekiel was just a few weeks old when he came with his two-year-old sister, Vumileah. Their father had died weeks earlier, tragically shortly followed by their mother. Their grandfather brought them to us saying that he was about to remarry and asked us to take them for six months and that he would return for them, whereupon his new wife would care for them. They lived about 20 km away in the countryside. The children were left with their new grandmother who was only in her early forties. The grandfather still worked in the city and visited the family regularly, which is a very common situation in Burundi. About six months passed and the grandfather came to tell us that Vumileah had died and Ezekiel was ailing. We visited them to assess the situation and found that the children had been severely neglected. Vumileah had died as a result of malnourishment and malaria and Ezekiel looked as if he was suffering from the same conditions. We brought him back and took him to hospital. Miraculously he recovered and he joined us in the CRIB family. Ezekiel graduates this year. He will be taking an online Montessori teaching diploma course and will start work as a trainee infant teacher in the infant section of our school.

Niyongarbo was brought to us by his father after his mother had died giving birth. Niyo is halfway through his A levels and his plan is to study medicine. He is very bright and focused and is one of our top students. He will make an excellent doctor.

John Paul was six weeks old when his teenage sister, Fabiola, arrived on our doorstep with him. He weighed just 3 kg and looked like a skeleton with skin on. I very much doubted when I saw this baby that he would survive. His sister had kept him alive for those six weeks since their mother died after delivery. We took in both Fabiola and John Paul and began the long, slow process of trying to treat his extensive dehydration and starvation problems. He slowly started to respond and thankfully began to gain weight; he started to look like a real baby rather than a skeleton. John Paul is due to graduate from school this summer and has an internship with an organization in Burundi where he will learn about tourism. He plans to get a job as a tour guide, which he will be very good at on account of his personable and adventurous personality!

Jessie was a few days old when he arrived. He had been found lying in a ditch next to a woman who had been killed (probably his mother). We have never been able to find out about or trace any of his relatives. Jessie is almost eighteen and about to graduate from school, hopefully with good enough grades to go on to do A levels. He doesn't yet know what he would like to do career-wise.

Isaiah came to CRIB after his mother died. He was only a few weeks old. Isaiah was in his teens when we discovered his father was still alive as well as two other siblings and an aunt. He visits them during the school holidays. Isaiah is nearly eighteen years old and hopes to be able to go on to do A levels. He would like to be a civil engineer.

Francois came to us at eleven months old. Having been abandoned by his mother, he came to CRIB with severe scoliosis and was very unhappy. But after several months with us, the children gathered to pray for him, and he made a remarkable recovery – his back was *completely* straight. Within a few days he was taking his first steps and he has never looked back. He is now seventeen and has one more year to do in school before he graduates, and at this point, he has no idea what he wants to do in the future. One thing is very sure: God has a plan for Francois's life.

Olivier arrived as a baby. He had been orphaned with no known relatives. Oli has had his share of challenges over the years. He has quite severe learning difficulties but he is very gifted in practical work. He loves doing anything with woodwork and we hope to be able to find a good placement where he can learn a trade, maybe carpentry.

Kosami also came as a new baby following the death of his mama after delivery. He does still have a father who has since remarried and Kosami goes to stay with them during the school holidays. He is coming to the end of Year 9 so has a couple of years left to think about his IGCSEs and what he wants to do in the future.

Clavere is one of our youngest boys and has been with us since he was a baby. He still has a few years of school left and is halfway through Year 7 in secondary school.

Claude, who has been with us since he was a baby, is also just about to finish Year 7 and does not yet know what he would like to do in the future.

Jacob was a few months old when he arrived as an orphan. Jacob, Clavere, and Claude are all close friends. When one is in trouble, we almost certainly find the other two close behind!

Gideon was orphaned at one day old. He will graduate this year. Gideon loves gardening and is especially interested in learning about landscape gardening and the cultivation of flowers.

Andrew is the most amazing soccer player. I think we are all convinced that he could be a professional soccer player but it is not that easy to be spotted by a scout in Burundi. Andrew has struggled a little with academic work at school but excels at sport. He will graduate from school next year and besides his passion for football, he doesn't know what career he will pursue yet.

Elijah was orphaned with no known relatives. He has another two years in school before he graduates and has no firm ideas of what he wants to do in the future.

Freddie is coming to the end of Year 7 and is a real character. He is not particularly academic but is excellent at practical tasks around the house.

Edward came to us with his twin sister when they were both a few months old. Their mother had died and their father could not cope with twin babies. Edward and his sister are both dyslexic so struggle with school work. He is also good at sport, particularly football and would like to train as a motor mechanic. He is very close to his twin sister and is currently just finishing Year 8.

Ciza and Able are two brothers who arrived with their teenage sister **Nizigiyimana** after their mother died. Able was just a few hours old and still had the umbilical cord attached. However, he possessed a pair of very healthy lungs, which he used to good effect when he entered our CRIB home! Ciza was almost twenty months old when he arrived. He was very quiet and withdrawn. He was found to have protein deficiency malnutrition and malaria and was hospitalized. After a week, Nizigiyimana, who, in the absence of any known living relatives, had been caring for him in the hospital, came back to join Able at CRIB. It was a few years later that an opportunity came for this family to be adopted by some friends, who pastor a church in California. It was an amazing journey to process the adoption. It took several years to complete but eventually God made a way and these three young adults are all doing remarkably well. They have been back to visit us a few times and I visit them every couple of years when I am in the USA.

Dale, Amy, and their church family are committed to helping the whole of our CRIB family and have been generous financially and in sending teams during the summer months to organize camps for the children.

The Girls

Fabiola walked about 20 km from up in the countryside with her six-week-old brother, John Paul. She came to the city after their mother had died giving birth to her baby brother. She herself had malaria, typhoid, and was also very malnourished. It was amazing that either of them survived that trek. After the right medical treatment, Fabiola started school and did very well. She eventually went to Uganda for two years to take A-levels, and then completed a Montessori course online once she had returned to Burundi.

Today Fabiola has a degree in Leadership, which she gained by teaching during the day and then going to classes in the evening. She is now teaching art and music in our primary school. She also has a vision to open a dance studio in Burundi one day. Since coming to CRIB, she discovered that her father and two sisters were still alive and were living in the city. Fabiola and John Paul see them often. Fabs is now renting a small apartment in town and is completely independent; she is a survivor! An amazing testimony of God's grace and goodness.

We spoke about **Grace** in an earlier chapter, but her amazing story of survival and God's hand on her life is worth repeating here. Having been found in a public toilet in one of the city hospitals she came to CRIB at five days old. We discovered she was deaf at around eight months old. After she was prayed for and anointed with oil, she was miraculously healed of that deafness. She is now studying at university in the USA and hopes to be a journalist. I would not be surprised if she writes her own story one day: a story of God's faithfulness against all human odds.

Belize came to us when she was about a year old. Her mother had died soon after delivery and her grandmother had been looking after her. However, she was now too old and sick to care for her. Belize lived at CRIB until she was fifteen years old and then went to live with her cousin. She continued to attend The King's School, though, and travelled by bus every day, having lunch with us at CRIB, and returning home each evening. She recently graduated from school and started a three-year college diploma course in Burundi. She is doing very well and CRIB will continue to support her until she has completed the diploma and finds employment.

Leah was about eighteen months old when she was found abandoned in a cardboard box under a tree. Her medical check-up showed she had an enlarged liver, was very anaemic, and HIV positive. We loved her, prayed for her, and fed her with a high-protein diet, and she slowly began to improve.

It was months before she started to move her legs and attempted to stand up, then eventually to walk. Leah started school at five and was eating well with her health remaining stable. However, it became obvious that she had learning difficulties, which proved to be a great frustration for her as she just couldn't get the hang of reading. Other than that, she did well until her early teenage years when she had to start anti-viral treatment for HIV.

Leah was a delight. She saw life in simple terms and didn't really understand what HIV was or really meant. She had dreams and desires like all young girls but her biggest ambition was to live to be eighteen years old. After a period of being unwell, shortly before her twentieth birthday, Leah died. She just laid her head back on the pillow and left us. She had decided that that was the day that she was to meet her Lord.

Oscalina was four months old when her uncle brought her to CRIB. Her mother had died two weeks earlier and Oscalina had only been fed with black tea and water since then. She was understandably very malnourished. Over time, she started to recover and did well. She is now in her final year at school and will graduate next year. She is currently considering in what direction she would like to go in the future.

Janine, at four months old, had been found abandoned next to the body of a woman whom we assumed had been her mother. We took Janine in but a few months later a lady turned up who said she was Janine's mother. She had a large wound on her head and was paralysed down one of her arms. She said she had fled her attackers and wanted to take Janine back. She had not seen her husband for a few weeks after the attack but had now been reunited with him. With husband and baby found, she wanted to start life again. It was a challenge to let Janine go as her mother did not look strong enough to be able to care for her but, after all, Janine was her child and she convinced us that she had help at home.

It was quite a few weeks later that she returned with Janine, who now looked malnourished and unkempt. Her mother bravely admitted that she couldn't cope as her husband had had to leave to find work and she was bringing Janine back to us so that we could give her the help and care she needed. Suffice to say, Janine stayed at CRIB for good this time.

Today, Janine is a healthy happy teenager about to graduate from school and start a college diploma in Burundi. Her parents separated and now live in different areas of Burundi, but Janine still sees them from time to time. Janine is a born leader!

Alida came to CRIB when she was four months old after her mother died from malaria. She weighed only about 3.5 kg and was very malnourished. Alida responded well to good food and a lot of TLC at CRIB, but then suddenly, after about three months had passed, she became ill very quickly. We took her to hospital where she was eventually diagnosed with meningitis. She remained in hospital for weeks as they were unable to control her high fever and continual convulsions. It looked unlikely that she would survive.

When she came home, Alida was paralysed from the neck down and seemed to be blind and possibly deaf. Her quality of life was very poor and she was allocated a Mama just for herself to look after her. She used to enjoy a cup of tea and fruit and yoghurt.

Alida lived to be eighteen years old before God took her home in early 2015.

Maria was five months old when she was brought to CRIB by her old grandfather who was unable to look after her. Both her parents were dead.

Over the years, Maria has enjoyed life and done well at school. She will graduate from school this year. She is gifted in hairdressing and is very skilled in braiding hair. However, Maria would like to train to be a nurse and maybe do hairdressing as a sideline!

Joy was just twenty-four hours old when she arrived at CRIB. Her mother had died in childbirth and Joy was one of nine children. Joy has enjoyed being at CRIB and visits her siblings occasionally. At the present time, she is in her last year at school and is undecided about what she wants to do in the future.

Beth is coming up to her last year in The King's School. She came to us at four weeks old. She is still thinking about what she wants to do as a career.

Delayida has a twin brother, Edward. Both have challenges with dyslexia and have struggled at school. Delayida is coming to the end of Year 9 at school and is thinking about what she would like to do in the future.

Esther was a beautiful baby when she came to us at four months old. She is due to graduate from school this year. She would like to go on to do A levels so that she can train to be a psychologist.

Ruth was found wrapped in a blanket in the car park of a restaurant. We estimated her age to be about four months old. However, she looked healthy and had been well cared for. She is now a teenager, is doing well at school, and is due to graduate next year.

Darhlene's mother died when she was only four days old, and was brought to us at three weeks old. She currently has to complete one more year at school. She is undecided about her future career at this point.

Estella came to CRIB when she was about eight months old. She was living in a refugee camp with her three-year-old brother after their mother had died. Her brother was old enough to eat normal food and so was taken in by an aunt and Estella was brought to CRIB. She has one more year to complete before she graduates from school, and loves all things sporty, particularly football, volleyball, and tennis. She still visits her brother and aunt during school holidays.

Kwizera arrived from a refugee camp one New Year's Eve, aged only a month old. Her mother had died and she had no one to care for her. She has one more year left at school before she graduates.

Ornella was six months old when she arrived. Her mother died as a result of being hit by a car, but Ornella, who was strapped to her back at the time, was fortunately unhurt. She has been part of the CRIB family ever since.

Anna-Carleen was brought to us by a medical student who was working at the hospital where her mother had died. She was a healthy looking and well cared for baby. Currently she has two more years before she graduates from The King's School.

Angela was another baby rescued from a refugee camp. She was five months old when she arrived. Her mother was very sick with malaria and was unable to cope with a baby. Angela also had malaria. She has just two more years left before she graduates from school.

Esperance was about sixteen months old when she came to us. A neighbour had found her after her mother had been killed. "Supe" was very traumatized when she arrived but quickly settled and has done well, despite some ongoing health problems. She is very sociable and has many friends.

Rebecca was eighteen months old when she was brought to us late one evening. She had been found abandoned and had badly burned feet and legs. It looked as if a pot of water had accidentally been tipped over her from a charcoal fire – a very common occurrence in Burundi as food is traditionally cooked in pots outside on charcoal fires. She is now a teenager and has a year left before she graduates from school.

Euodia was about five days old when she arrived as a tiny but healthy looking, beautiful baby. Euodia has struggled with school and has to work hard to understand everything. She is behind others in her age group academically and it will be a few years before she is able to graduate from school. She may well go on to undertake some practical training in the future.

Nizigiyimana was eleven years old when she arrived with her two brothers, Ciza and Able. This family are now living in California with their adoptive parents, Dale and Amy. I am still their Mama Chrissie, so proud of them and grateful to their new parents for loving them and opening their hearts and homes to these children.

In the weeks before these children were adopted, after years of believing their whole family had been killed, it was discovered that their grandmother and another brother were still alive. It was wonderful for them to be able to meet and talk before they left Burundi.

For many who read this list of names and their stories, it may merely represent a group of children who have survived a horrendous genocide. To me, and to all those who have worked at CRIB, we know that each of them has a tailor-made plan fashioned by their heavenly Father. That is what we have told these young people over the years. We pray that they will choose to do the best that they can with what they have and to fulfil their destiny.

In the midst of this poverty-stricken African nation with all that life has thrown at them, this group of young people are the next generation who will be a part of Burundi's future. They have been raised in an atmosphere of love, not hate, and introduced to Jesus. We have taught them that it is only in Him they can find true freedom and forgiveness. They can walk tall knowing that they have a heavenly Father who loves them and has a plan for their lives. They also have each other – many brothers and sisters. Some have surviving family members and in time may return to Burundi and build relationships with them. They have me. I am their Mama Chrissie. I do not have any plans to leave Burundi or my children. I would one day like to meet some of the grandchildren!

Rosa and Deo – what a wonderful couple: called to be missionaries in their own country. They have given their lives to help raise these children with me. Rosa and Deo are also like my children. God has given us destiny together.

Libby, who came as a teenager to help at CRIB, married a national and they have three children of their own. Not only are they fully committed to the young people at CRIB, but they also have a ministry to street children in Burundi.

There are also many people who have passed through CRIB who have had a significant impact in the lives of these children. There are hundreds more who have never been to Burundi but have given financially and therefore sowed into the ministry. We will never really know how many lives have been touched because of this faithful giving. I have had the privileged position of being a channel for all that is given.

It is humbling to know that this is what I was born for: for Africa and its orphans and widows. I am Mama to fifty-three of the most awesome young people you will ever hope to meet. Some of these youngsters may eventually live in other countries around the world, but I believe that most of them will settle in Burundi and make a difference to their country of birth. There are still an estimated one million orphans in this country and the numbers grow daily. There is so much need and so much that needs doing. We continue to do what we can with what we have. We act as a channel by distributing food and offering medical help and care whenever people come to us.

It is quite daunting to stop and think about the finance we are going to need to facilitate the next step in the lives of these fifty-three young people. I know for sure the same God who has provided for all our needs over the years will continue to provide. My testimony is that we have always had enough. I have travelled too far, experienced too much, and seen God at work so often to think that these children are where they today just because of human intervention. They have survived because of Jesus. We are merely *His* vessels.

We are called to be extraordinary and because of Jesus we can walk in the fullness of the life He has called us to live and be the people He has called us to be. When we are living in the centre of God's will we open the way to be a blessing to others.

I feel that one day there will be another book, another story, maybe written by one of the CRIB children who will chronicle the next stage of their journeys. I wonder how many doctors, lawyers, nurses, musicians, teachers, carpenters, or mechanics will come out of CRIB? I am sure there will be leaders among this group. Maybe we have one who could one day lead the nation. Who knows?

As I come to the end of this book, I remember a vision I had many years ago. I stood in my living room, gazing at all the babies lying in rows on beanbags. It was as if the room became larger all of a sudden and I saw the babies as adults. I knew that there were those in that room who would hold significant positions in Burundi.

I recently came across words from American pastor Andy Stanley that really impacted me: "Your greatest contribution to the kingdom of God may not be something that you do, but rather someone you raise."

I cannot complete this book without talking about the faithfulness of God. We can sometimes be quick to quote a verse of Scripture to help a friend in trouble or to give encouragement. We can sometimes pull a verse out of the Bible like a rabbit out of a hat. We deliver our verse and hope it will do the trick and provide some comfort. Sometimes the depth of the challenge seems to make the situation worse. Some of the experiences I have faced in Burundi have caused me to look deeper and to ask uncomfortable questions. How do you tell a young mother who has lost her husband, her home, and everything she owns in this life that there is still hope? She is malnourished and stands holding her newborn baby but has no milk to feed this precious little life. How do you tell her that all things work together for good? She loves God but things do not seem to have worked together for good. Are we allowed to ask such questions of the Lord?

I remember a few years ago sitting in a doctor's office waiting for the results of the biopsy on the lump on my breast. I don't think I will ever forget the feeling in the pit of my stomach when the doctor looked me in the eye and said he was sorry to tell me I had cancer – not just in one breast but in both. Within three days of that diagnosis, I was in hospital for a double mastectomy.

At the time I was diagnosed, three other friends were also battling the same disease and none of them were doing well. People were praying for me. Some sent cards with verses of encouragement – "God is faithful" was a favourite. However, at that particular time, I did not feel that He was. I prayed to find three different couples who would be willing to take Lydia, Hannah, and Ben if the worst was to happen. As I struggled and battled for weeks with all the "what ifs" while I waited to hear back if the cancer had spread, most of all I feared what would happen to my children. How could God let this happen to me? Am I wrong to ask those questions? My questions were eventually answered with another question. How do you know that God is faithful unless you are able to prove His faithfulness? I proved God's faithfulness somewhere in that pit of distress and darkness; I came to the realization that cancer was not my enemy, but fear. Fear of the unknown. Fear of the "what ifs". I had to consciously decide to give all my fears to Him and trust that His plans were perfect, even if it didn't feel like it. Somehow it was as if the faithfulness of God embraced me in choosing to trust Him. I came out the other side of that experience not just believing that God is faithful because that is what it says in the Bible, but because I experienced it.

He has a perfect plan and it is not for me to work it out but to keep trusting and believing that all things do work together for good. The faithfulness of God is not something we know intellectually or have been taught: it is to be experienced, embraced, and lived in.

As I look into the eyes of each of the CRIB children, I can see the living, breathing proof of God's faithfulness at work.

EPILOGUE

Life moves on and during the months I have spent writing this book, Burundi has undergone yet another upheaval which has brought about many changes for us.

In June 2015, after struggling with serious health problems for years, our precious Alida went to sleep and never woke up. I think she had decided she wanted to be with Jesus instead.

Unfortunately, none of the students that were due to graduate in the summer of 2015 had the chance to do so. The fact that this country stands on the brink of civil war meant that all such plans were curtailed. A week into the final school term after the Easter break came the announcement that Burundi's president planned to run for election for a controversial third term in office. This news was followed by an uprising from many who were in opposition. An attempted coup followed.

This has resulted in an estimated 300,000 people fleeing the country in fear of their lives into neighbouring Rwanda, Congo, and Tanzania. The refugee camps once again are swollen with desperate people and the aid agencies are overwhelmed with the sheer volume of people arriving daily. Food is in short supply and cholera has taken so many lives, especially the children who are weak and vulnerable from the miles they have had to walk to what they hoped would be a place of safety. This is heartbreaking.

Not surprisingly, the foreign embassies in Burundi advised non-essential personnel to leave the country immediately.

For months now we have had to listen to the sound of grenades, bombs and gunfire throughout the night. News reporting is not allowed at the moment.

For me, I have an overwhelming sense of déjà vu. Dozens of people have been killed and the feeling of tension is almost palpable. I fear that at any time things will bubble over and war will once again break out. Meanwhile, we wait and pray.

Leaving the country was never an option for me. God has given me responsibility for the lives of so many young people and employees and I am not going to abandon them. In any event, where would we all go?

We continue to pray for this beautiful country that God will somehow intervene and bring us back to a place of peace and stability. More than once I have been reminded of the angels who protected us all those years ago. How amazing it is that I have spent several months recalling those events to record in this book. I am filled with such an assurance that the same God who protected us then, who sent those angelic beings to stand guard on our walls, is the same God who will protect and provide for us. He will lead and guide us as we continue to put our trust in Him.

As I write, life is a challenge here in Burundi. Food is in short supply and has doubled in price overnight. Fuel for our vehicles is scarce (and difficult to find) and we have frequent water and electricity cuts, sometimes lasting days.

However, in all these hardships, I can say God is faithful. He has continued to provide for our needs and we have always managed to get enough to eat and have never completely run out of fuel.

Who knows what lies ahead in the forthcoming weeks, months, years? God's plans are perfect and He will fulfil everything he has planned. He is not taken by surprise by anything – neither by wars nor rumours of wars.

As the apostle Paul wrote in 2 Corinthians 4:18:

> *So we don't look at the troubles we can see now; rather, we fix our gaze on things that cannot be seen. For the things we see now will soon be gone, but the things we cannot see will last forever.*

And we give Him all the glory.

What a *mighty* God we serve!

Chrissie Chapman
September 2015

ABOUT THE AUTHOR

I was born in Stockport, Cheshire, which is in the north of England. My parents were good working class people; my mother was a cook and my father was a motor mechanic. My sister and I shared a bedroom in the small council house that we rented. I was not an exceptionally bright child, however, and the school that I attended was not an illustrious institution and was given the nickname "graffiti city" by the locals!

I struggled throughout my teenage years with health and weight issues and suffered quite badly with asthma, polycystic ovary syndrome and quite an extensive range of allergics. Over the years I was to spend quite a lot of time in hospital and on more than one occasion, came closer to death than was comfortable. One constant that remained in my life at that time was that I wanted to be a midwife. I love babies and have always loved babies and had a plan that one day I would have about a dozen! Little did I know what lay ahead…

At the age of nineteen I was accepted on a three-year nursing course; quite a miracle as I had such a bad medical history and no real educational qualifications. However, I passed the entrance exam and after three years qualified as a State Registered Nurse. I worked for a few years in various hospitals in and around Manchester and then moved to Epsom (which is just outside London) where at last I was able to realize my dream of training to be a midwife.

One thing that seems to characterize my life is that things never seem to be straightforward. I experienced love and great loss at a very early age. My health was a constant challenge. When I completed my midwifery training and went on holiday to France with some friends, I unfortunately got drunk one night and went swimming and knocked myself out on an anchored boat. I ended up being flown back to the UK by air ambulance. It was as I sat again in yet another hospital bed that I realized I could have died. The doctor who treated me just happened to be a Christian and started talking to me about Jesus. As I listened, I was led into the open arms of God where I found the love and acceptance I had craved all my life.

I had been to Sunday school as a child and even dipped in and out of church as a teenager, but was never really deeply committed to anything very much; but this time it was different. On this occasion I had an encounter with Jesus that made me want to change my life. It was a few years later when, after a number of serious asthmatic attacks, I had another near death experience. I once again ended up in hospital and this time suffered a respiratory arrest, I stopped breathing and was in the intensive care unit on a life support machine. I was not completely sure how long I was on that machine, but it was quite some time. I eventually woke up and realized that my lungs were in a pretty bad way. I had been given very large doses of steroids which had caused all my joints to swell. I had a condition called capsulitis and the joints in my neck had swollen and trapped a nerve causing excruciating pain. I had also lost sensation on the right side of my body. To add insult to injury, a lot of my hair had fallen out and in parts I was completely bald. I felt like I was dying and I wanted to die. Not long after this, one of the doctors I had become friendly with told me that I probably would die.

I hadn't really been a Christian all that long. I had read a lot of books on the subject of healing, but I never really saw anybody who had been healed of anything more than a headache or a bad back and I was quite cynical and thought that they probably would have got better anyway. So my conclusion was that God only healed people who could write books! I was sitting on the side of my hospital bed one day when I heard an audible voice say, "It's time to go home because I'm going to heal you." I had never experienced anything like this before but I was convinced that this was God and I grew excited and felt hope starting to rise inside me. However, in the state of health I was in, I wondered how I was ever going to persuade anybody to let me leave the hospital. Fortunately, I did manage to talk to some friends and asked them if they would convince the medical staff to let me go home, even if it was just for a weekend. I wasn't sure how to explain what had happened and I felt that if I told the doctor that I was hearing voices about going home I may well get transferred to a psychiatric unit! As things went, I was obviously very unwell and I suppose in the end they didn't think there was much to lose so the doctors allowed me to go home with the proviso that if I needed to, I was to come straight back to the ward where a bed would be waiting.

So, on that Friday afternoon, my friends sat me in a wheelchair and pushed me down to the car and got me home. They took me to my little bedsit and I sat on a beanbag at the side of the bed, totally convinced that the minute they left, I was going to be miraculously healed. As the day went on, I realized I was still in a pretty bad way; my lungs were filling with fluid and I was gasping for breath. I started to wonder if I had misunderstood what God had said to me and that He had probably meant that it was time to go home to heaven where I would get my new heavenly body.

Never having seen anybody healed or even really fully believing that God could heal me, I sat and just waited, not quite knowing what to do. Again, I couldn't get the verse of Scripture out of my head that the pastor from my church had left for me while visiting me in hospital earlier that week. He had written out 1 Peter 2:24: "He himself bore our sins in his body on the tree, so that we might die to sins and live for righteousness; by His wounds, you have been healed" (NIV), and had put it inside my Bible. Sitting there in my bedsit, I had an overwhelming desire to get my Bible and read this verse again. I managed to crawl across my bedroom floor as there was still weakness on my right side and I got my Bible and sat and turned to read this Scripture. Something inside me was stirred to take hold of this verse and I found it became completely alive to me. All I can say is that I had an encounter with the Holy Spirit like I've never experienced either before or since. The first thing that happened to me was that I got a revelation that Jesus had done all the healing He was ever going to do 2,000 years ago on the cross. This verse said, "by His wounds, you have been healed". It was already done and was mine to embrace and not to work out in my mind.

Immediately, I got a tremendous sensation of pins and needles in my head and I put my hand up to my hair and it felt like a bristly brush. Some of the bald patches were actually growing! I got a mirror to see what was happening and to my amazement my lips were no longer blue and I looked pink and healthy. I sat on my beanbag, not really comprehending what was happening but over the course of the next twelve hours, I got complete feeling back in my side. My hair miraculously grew back to normal and by the next morning, my lungs were completely functional. There seemed to be no fluid and I could breathe in and out freely. With great joy, I danced before the Lord, completely healed and completely whole.

The next challenge was coming to terms with being healed! In all honesty, I had become quite secure in my ill health so I felt quite apprehensive about going back to the hospital to explain to them what had happened to me. The truth was, I didn't quite know what had happened to me. All I knew was that I left the hospital ward dying and here I was with what felt like new lungs; I felt like a completely new person.

On Monday, I went back to the hospital to return their wheelchair. I walked into the ward and stood leaning on this empty wheelchair for a bit of support as my knees were shaking quite badly. The doctors were in the middle of a ward round at the time but stopped and turned around to look at the spectacle. Two of the doctors walked towards me, one of them being the consultant who had treated me on the ward. With mouth agape, all he could say was, "Good grief, it's risen!" to which I replied, "You're not wrong." The other doctor was the one who had earlier told me that I was probably going to die. Oh course, he noticed a massive difference in me, having seen me only two days before, but it was the fact that my face was pink and I had hair where I had been bald that seemed to affect him. He reached out, not believing what he was seeing to touch my hair and as he reached out, he slid down and landed on his knees and started to speak in tongues. I didn't know what to do or what to say so I blurted out, "You can't do that … I don't think you're saved!" It occurred to me then that the reason that we need signs and wonders is that it is the signs that make people wonder about Jesus. It was the most amazing moment. I have since heard that that young doctor went to India to serve the Lord in later years.

Over the next few weeks, many of the staff became Christians in that hospital. It was the hospital I had worked at so the staff knew me and knew my medical history. After seeing me, many of them started to ask questions and saw the reality of what God had done in my life. I had the privilege of being able to talk to many people there and to lead them to the Lord.

From that day to this, I have never had an asthmatic attack. God has given me two new lungs. After this experience, I cried out to God and said, "I want my life to make a difference." I asked the Lord to take the life he had given back to me and to use me in any way I could be of service to Him. I can say with certainly that He has done that. He took my request and the door opened for me to go to Roffey Place Christian Training Centre for a year. During my time there, I met and worked with Revd Bob Gordon. He took me to Burundi as part of a team to an outreach and healing mission and there I met a young pastor called David Ndaruhutse who was the leader of the mission that I eventually went out to Burundi with. Between 1985 and 1990, I visited Burundi five times and in 1990, I went to Burundi to serve the Lord and I have been there ever since. September 2014 will be the start of my twenty-fifth year in Burundi and it has been one incredible journey.

If you would like to get in touch with Chrissie Chapman, to find out more or to give to the work of CRIB, she can be contacted on:

chrissiesbook@gmail.com